The Okapi

The Okapi

Mysterious Animal of Congo-Zaire

Susan Lyndaker Lindsey
Mary Neel Green
Cynthia L. Bennett

Illustrations by Mary Neel Green
Foreword by Jane Goodall

University of Texas Press ◁▷ Austin

Requests for permission to reproduce material from
this work should be sent to Permissions, University
of Texas Press, Box 7819, Austin, TX 78713-7819.

⊚ The paper used in this publication meets the
minimum requirements of American National Standard
for Information Sciences–Permanence of Paper for
Printed Library Materials, ANSI Z39.48-1984.

Lindsey, Susan Lyndaker, 1956–   .
    The Okapi : mysterious animal of Congo-Zaire / Susan
Lyndaker Lindsey, Mary Neel Green, Cynthia L. Bennett ;
illustrations by Mary Neel Green.
        p.   cm.
    Includes bibliographical references (p.   ) and index.
    ISBN 0-292-74706-3 (alk. paper).   ISBN 0-292-74701-1
(pbk. : alk. paper)
    1. Okapi—Congo (Democratic Republic)—Ituri Forest.
I. Green, Mary Neel.   II. Bennett, Cynthia L.   III. Title.

QL737.U56L54   1999
599.638–dc21   98-28740

Dedicated to okapi and those who care for and about them.
May each new generation appreciate all the secrets they have
to share.

Contents

A man is ethical only when life, as such, is sacred to him, that of plants and animals as that of his fellow men.

ALBERT SCHWEITZER

Foreword

When I was about seven years old I began to read the Doctor Doolittle books. I loved them all, but the one that really seized my imagination was about his expedition into Africa to return some circus animals to their native forests. Then, a couple of years later, I met and fell in love with Tarzan—not the movie star (Johnny Weissmuller, at the time), but the magnificent Lord of the Jungle as I imagined him from my reading of Edgar Rice Burroughs' books. And so, when I was about ten years old I already knew when I grew up I wanted to go to Africa, live with animals, and write books about them. And if, at that time, I could have chosen where I wanted to go most, I would unhesitatingly have picked the then Belgian Congo—the very heart of Darkest Africa. I was utterly fascinated by everything I had read about the rain forest (or jungle, as we called it) with its tangled vegetation and teeming animal life.

It was in 1960 that I began to study chimpanzees in the Gombe National Park (then the Gombe Stream Game Reserve) in what was formerly Tanganyika and is now Tanzania. That was the year the Belgian Congo gained its independence from Belgian colonial rule. Indeed, it was when I arrived in the port of Kigoma on the eastern shore of Lake Tanganyika on my way to Gombe that the first Belgian refugees began arriving over the lake from eastern Congo. From the beach in Gombe one can look out over the water and, in the rainy season when the air is clear, see on the western shore the forested hills of the Congo—the country that has always fascinated me.

Today, this huge country (which became Zaire when President Mobutu Sese Seko came to power in 1960, and has now, since Laurent Kabila seized power in 1997, become the Democratic Republic of Congo, or Congo-Zaire) is still largely unexplored. The tourist industry has not developed in Central Africa for a variety of reasons. Visitors have often been hassled at border crossings, airports, and so forth; travel to the few national parks has been difficult; and recently the political upheavals in the region along with the Ebola virus outbreak have daunted even those intrepid souls who love adventuring off the beaten track. The majority of tourists flock to eastern and southern Africa. And so Congo-Zaire—or Congo-Kinshasa as it is often called today—is still a land of mystery, of untamed wilderness. It is a country that holds an irresistible appeal for the intrepid field biologist, for without doubt, much remains to be discovered.

Congo-Zaire is the third largest country in Africa. It has the greatest areas of intact tropical rain forest and is the most biologically diverse country on the continent. It is home to more species of mammals, birds, and amphibians—and also, I am told, more varieties of swallowtail butterflies!—than anywhere else in Africa. It ranks second in the number of reptile and flowering plant species. Many of the plants and animals found in Congo-Zaire are endemic, found nowhere else in the world. Indeed, the country is a paradise for the naturalist, for many species there have not yet been described for science. But in order to uncover these as-yet-unknown marvels, it is first necessary to conserve their habitat. This book is about the shy and little-known okapi and the other inhabitants of the Ituri Forest. Like most of the rest of Africa, this forest, with its great diversity of flora and fauna, its complex ecosystem, is facing many threats from the relentlessly increasing human populations.

When I first went by boat along the eastern shores of Lake Tanganyika, lush forests tumbled down from the peaks of the Rift Escarpment to the crystal clear waters of the lake. There were a few fishing villages, little thatched huts and small clearings where some cassava and beans were grown. But on the whole there was unbroken chimpanzee habitat for mile upon mile—from the Zambian border northward to Bujumbura in Burundi. And if you climbed to the peak of the rift escarpment and looked to the east, there too the forests stretched out, an almost solid sea of green. Today it is different. The shoreline of the Gombe National Park looks the same, but it is only a ten-mile stretch. To the north and south the trees are virtually gone. If you climb the hills and look to the east, the story is the same. Human dwellings and cultivated fields press up to the boundaries of the park. The hills are steep and, with the tree cover gone, each rainy season sees more of the thin layer of topsoil eroded away. In many places the once lush country looks like a barren desert. The wild animals have gone. And this devastation also is due to the ever-increasing needs of the ever-expanding human population in the area, including the constant influx of refugees from Burundi and from eastern Congo-Zaire.

The frightening change that we have seen outside the park over the past fifteen to twenty years is not unique. Forests and woodlands—indeed, all types of natural habitat—are being destroyed or severely degraded all over the world. This applies to the once vast Ituri Forest of Congo-Zaire. The local human population has mushroomed. Mining operations and clear-cutting for agriculture have degraded the forest. The wild animal populations have been ruthlessly exploited by poachers, many of whom hunt to satisfy the demand for bushmeat—the flesh of wild animals—in nearby towns. Those hunters who practice subsistence hunting, taking only enough game to feed themselves and their families, have lived in harmony with nature for hundreds of years; now their means of survival is in danger as the number of wild animals has decreased in many places. Some animal species are close to extinction. This is true of the mysterious okapi of the Ituri Forest.

The okapi was first described by Western scientists almost a hundred years ago, but for a very long time absolutely nothing was known of its behavior in the wild. Its closest relative is the familiar giraffe of the savanna—how easy to study compared with the shy okapi in the dense forest. Fortunately the authors of this book felt the urgency of the situation. They have been inspired to use their talents to share with us not only fascinating facts about the natural history of the okapi but also, and most importantly, the need to save this extremely beautiful creature and the wondrous forest that is its home.

In this beautifully written and illustrated book we learn how, gradually, dedicated research has unveiled more and more of the secrets of okapi natural history. And we become increasingly fascinated by the utter magic of the forest, the complexity and interrelatedness of plant and animal life, and the part played by the indigenous people. You cannot read this book and not be moved by the thought that so much beauty, so many millions of years of evolution could yet be destroyed.

The authors have done the research and written this book because they care. They have donated their time and their skill to assisting the survival of the okapi. Publication of this book will provide an impetus to the efforts that are being made to maintain the Okapi Wildlife Reserve

within the Ituri Forest. This is a project that has involved both Westerners and Africans and is a project worth supporting.

I congratulate the authors for their passion and for their commit-
ment. They have not only cared, they have acted. They not only felt that
the okapi *should* be saved, they have taken steps to ensure that it *will* be
saved. Already they have advanced the cause, for this book will have long-
lasting effects on conservation of the okapi and preservation of the forest:
the authors' research will heighten awareness of the plight of the okapi,
and their royalties will go directly to the Ituri forest conservation program. You will be helping if you buy this book and encourage your
friends to do the same. Okapis have a special place in the natural world,
and it is up to us to ensure that they and their forests survive.

JANE GOODALL
1998

Acknowledgments

Large projects require lots of enthusiasm, encouragement, and support. We received all three in abundance. When the idea of a book about the natural history of the okapi was first presented to Warren Iliff and Dr. Ron Kagan, then director and general curator, respectively, at the Dallas Zoo, they encouraged us to move forward with this endeavor. And how did each of us move this project, so soon to take wing, from thought to reality? Mary Neel Green's original idea was first shared in muted tones with Susan Lyndaker Lindsey in the okapi barn, with an audience of okapi looking on. Like Susan, Cynthia L. Bennett had been concentrating her research on the okapi, and both had grown very interested in helping to preserve and support this unique animal. Mary Neel's considerable artistic talent was often glimpsed during her long stays in the okapi barn while assisting with the research. Even through a job change and a move, Susan never lost optimism about the project. Mary Neel never gave up despite delays and sent along new art work and historical information to inspire additional prose. Along the way we were encouraged and supported by that essential abundance of others.

Dallas Zoo staff helped in any way they could. Our thanks go to the City of Dallas, the Dallas Zoological Society, and Fred LaRue, Ken Kaemmerer, Charles Siegel, Wanda Weaver, Gena Wilson, Janelle Barron, and Norman Piwonka in particular. Animal care staff who furnished needed information included Dave Wilson, Sherry Mossbarger, Elizabeth Pyle Stolze, Mark Willow, Angela Yang Fry, and Gena Dodson. A special thank you is extended to Lisa Fitzgerald, who never wavered in her support, and to docent Rick Vidal for his translation skills.

Dr. Robert Weise, then with the American Zoo and Aquarium Association office; Dr. Barney Lipscomb, Collection Manager of the Botanical Research Institute of Texas; Dr. Herbert Robbins, Professor of Biology at Dallas Baptist University; Steve Shurter of White Oak Conservation Center in Florida; Ann Petric of Chicago Zoological Park in Brookfield; John and Terese Hart of Wildlife Conservation International; Karl and Rosemarie Ruf of GIC Epulu Project; horticulturist Tina Dombrowsky; lepidopterist Ernest F. Ryan and veterinarians Dr. Bonnie Raphael of the International Wildlife Conservation Park in New York; Dr. Tom Alvarado of the Dallas Zoo; and Dr. Kathryn Gamble, also of the Dallas Zoo, all willingly shared their expertise. Bruno Van Puijenbroeck and Kristin Leus of the Royal Zoological Society of Antwerp were very helpful in the final stages of this project. We are very grateful to Dr. Jane Goodall for her unparalleled contribution. We also appreciate the assistance of Judge Oswin Chrisman and Teresa Generous.

The necessary job of proof reading was handled by Jim Baldwin, April Woods, and Dr. Herbert Robbins. The manuscript was much improved by the input of several readers, including Ann Petric, Steve Shurter, and John Hart. At different stages of the project Sherry Pettijohn, Todd Pettijohn, Cynthia Pettit, George B. Green, Jr., Kevin Lindsey and Ryan Lindsey provided just the help that was needed.

Since illustrations would be of primary importance in telling the story of the okapi, we asked the volunteers and keepers of the Dallas Zoo to share their photographic skills. In particular we need to acknowledge the portfolio of Elizabeth Pyle Stolze and photos from Gena Dodson, Mary Margaret Underkofler, Naomi Henderson, Darla Brodsky, Julie Evans, Jan McKenney, and Mackie Harper. These photos, along with many we took, provided a large base of poses from which to draw. Some commercial photos were used as inspiration for depicting a particular behavior. Most of all, the extensive okapi collection of the Dallas Zoo provided ample material and inspiration.

For those who encouraged us by just being interested in our project and who took the time to ask, "How's the okapi book coming?" we would like to say thank you. Your interest often reminded us that for those who care about okapi and the Ituri rain forest animals, this was a story that had to be shared. Without all those who so willingly helped us, we would never have been able to complete this book on one of the most charismatic animals discovered in the twentieth century—the okapi.

Finally, on behalf of the multitude of globally important species that inhabit the most biologically diverse area in Africa, we thank you for assisting in its preservation through the purchase of this book.

The Okapi

1. Introduction

Emerald foliage hangs like a thick textured curtain, making it difficult to enter, but once one is within the rain forest, the shade provides a welcome relief from the equatorial sun. Ground vegetation thins and movement becomes easier. High overhead, the leaf canopy spreads, resembling a shimmering stained-glass window held in place by thick, tall tree trunks. Smaller young trees reach up toward the distant sun. An earthy, rich smell dominates the stagnant, humid air, but every so often, there is the faint, sweet fragrance of a nearby blooming plant.

The rain forest is alive with the varied sounds of many birds, the whirr of insects, and the calls of unseen primates. At the base of a huge tree a large russet-colored animal silently browses, using its long tongue to reach up into the trees for leaves. Suddenly the animal freezes as if listening to something. With a crash, a large branch falls from an adjacent tree, and instantly the animal disappears into the Ituri Forest.

Male okapi browsing Ricinodendron heudelotii, which the natives call "peke."

Young okapi standing in vegetation.

For decades stories circulated about unusual animals in the dark jungle at the center of Africa. Such lore was probably inspired by Phillip Gosse's book, *The Romance of Natural History,* published in 1861. He speculated that those animals yet to be discovered would be found in central Africa. Gosse thought that this might include the unicorn because natives in the Congo had told him about a horned animal they called "abada." Imaginations were stirred. It would be two decades before this particular mystery would be solved.

While exploring the Congo between 1882 and 1886, Wilhelm Junker, a wealthy physician, received an unusual piece of striped skin from an animal the people of the area called "makapi." Not realizing the importance of the unidentified skin, he decided that this animal must be a musk deer.

In June of 1889, a French army officer's journal of a trip in central Africa described in detail a beautiful animal seen along a river bank. Captain Jean Baptise Marchand saw a timid animal that appeared ready to run at any second, while other animals nearby were only curious. The captain did not find this animal mentioned in any zoological literature; he decided that it might be an antelope.

The most authentic information about the mystery animal came from Sir Henry Morton Stanley. He had made his first trip to Africa in 1871 for the *New York Herald* in order to search for Dr. David Livingston, a missionary who had disappeared three years earlier. Following his famous encounter with Dr. Livingston, Stanley spent many years exploring Africa, commissioned by King Leopold II of Belgium. In his book *In Darkest Africa*, published in 1890, Stanley wrote in an appendix, "The Wambutti (these dwarfs) knew a donkey and called it 'Atti.' They say that they sometimes catch them in pits. What they can find to eat is a wonder. They eat leaves." Although Stanley had never seen an "atti," his brief mention of the creature became a fortuitous step toward solution of the mystery when it attracted the attention of Sir Harry Johnston. Prior to assuming the office of governor of the British Protectorate of Uganda in 1899, Johnston spoke with Stanley in person about his interest in the

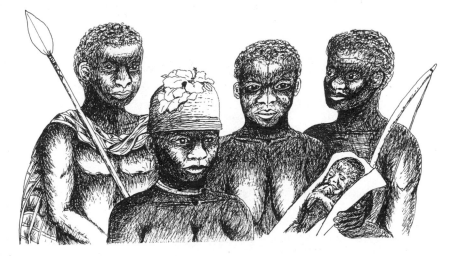

Mbuti pygmies.

"atti." Stanley related to Johnston that he and his men had only occasion-ally caught a glimpse of the animal while traveling in the Congo on the west side of the Semliki River, which flows from Lake Albert to Lake Edward. Johnston was determined to obtain a skin and learn as much about the "atti" as he could.

In 1900 several Mbuti pygmies (a term often used for the world's shortest people, derived from a Greek word meaning "half an arm's length") were kidnapped by a German impresario who wanted to display them at the Paris World's Fair. The Belgian government of the Congo sought Johnston's help when the smugglers fled to Uganda. Johnston agreed to see that the Mbuti hunters were returned to their home in the Ituri Forest. While they were in his care, he talked to them about Stanley's "atti." The natives told Johnston that there was a large animal in their forest that looked like a donkey with stripes. They called it "o'api." Johnston won-dered, since it had stripes, if this was a forest zebra.

Grant's zebra.

It was several months before Johnston was able to return the Mbuti to their home in the Ituri. On the way, he stopped at Fort Mbeni in the Semliki Forest, a post commanded by Lieutenant Meura. When questioned about this animal, the Belgian told him that there was a skin somewhere in the camp. It had been cut up by the soldiers of the Bambuba tribe to make bandoliers and belts. Two of the bandoliers were given to Johnston. The Bambuba called the striped animal "okapi."

Johnston was so excited about finding additional evidence that this animal existed that he organized an expedition immediately. Some of the Mbuti were his guides. As they traveled the forest paths, the Mbuti would point out the tracks of the "o'api." They were not at all what Johnston expected. Zebras, donkeys, and horses had one toe or hoof on each foot, but this animal was cloven-hooved, possessing two toes on each foot. He suspected the Mbuti might be misleading him intentionally.

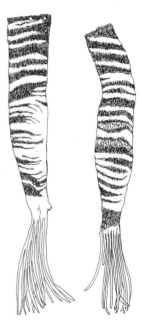

After a few days, Johnston had to abandon his search because his party came down with malaria. Belgian soldiers assisted Johnston's expedition in their return to Uganda. He was very disappointed that he had not seen or caught an "o'api." Lieutenant Meura promised to send him a whole skin. Immediately upon returning to Uganda, Johnston sent the pieces of skin (the bandoliers) he had received at Fort Mbeni to Europe for identification. It was October, 1900.

Sometime in November, Dr. P. L. Sclater, secretary of the Zoological Society of London, opened a diplomatic bag. It held a letter and two strips of brown and white striped skin. The letter stated that the "bandoliers" were made by native soldiers from the skin of an unknown animal. Dr. Sclater had never before seen such a skin. He immediately examined the strips under a microscope and found that the hair appeared to be similar to that of the zebra and the giraffe, but different from that of the

Okapi-skin bandoliers (redrawn from Lankester 1902b).

antelope. Intrigued, he first exhibited them at the December 18, 1900, meeting of the London Zoological Society.

Newspapers soon circulated the news that evidence of a new, large, living animal had been discovered in Africa. Rumors and speculations began to fly across Europe and America. Was this a concocted tale? Was this animal a hoax? How could an animal this large go undetected for so long?

If the stories were true, what kind of an animal could it be? It was supposed to have ears like a donkey. Perhaps it was a type of horse or donkey? It was said to have stripes. Maybe it was a forest zebra? Others thought that it could be a type of antelope or musk deer. Could it be the fabled unicorn, mentioned in ancient Greek and Roman writings? Some thought it might be a "missing link" to an ancient animal that lived thousands of years ago.

Europe, deep in its colonial heritage, was enthralled with the idea of new exotic lands, people, plants, and animals. What were their explorers and merchants going to bring home next for them to see and buy? When would they get to see this new sensation?

The new animal was named *Equus johnstoni* at a February 5, 1901, meeting of the Zoological Society of London because scholars thought it was most likely a new zebra species.

*   *   *

Meanwhile back in Uganda, Johnston waited for more information from Lieutenant Meura about the "o'api." Unfortunately, shortly after making his promise to Johnston, the lieutenant died of black-water fever. However, the second-in-command, Lieutenant Karl Erikson, a Scandinavian, followed through, and in February 1901 sent Johnston a skin and skull from one animal, plus an additional smaller skull. In the enclosed note he described the hooves as being bluish-black in color, like those of an antelope—and cloven.

When Johnston received the skulls in April, he made a fascinating discovery. To his surprise the "o'api" was not a horse, zebra, or antelope. From the shape of the skull and teeth, its nearest relative appeared to be the giraffe. He thought perhaps it was a descendant of an ancient giraffid, such as the *Helladotherium* that lived in Asia and Europe several million years ago. Apparently, no one had thought that this secretive resident of the Ituri Forest could be a giraffe. The skin and skulls were sent to England accompanied by a letter and a watercolor of what Johnston thought two living "o'api" would look like—even though he had yet to see one.

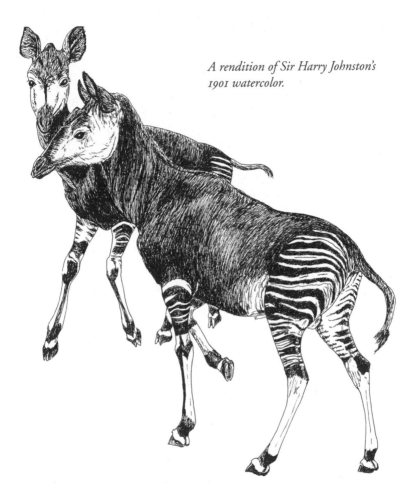

A rendition of Sir Harry Johnston's 1901 watercolor.

Sir Harry Johnston's second package arrived in London, causing as much excitement as the first. At the May 7, 1901, meeting of the Zoological Society, the two skulls and the skin were displayed. Johnston was present at the June 8, 1901, meeting to give a narrative of the discovery of the "o'api." He suggested that its scientific name be *Helladotherium tigrunum*;

tigrunum because of the animal's white stripes. Later that year and after much study, Sir E. Ray Lankester, director of the British Museum of Natural History, proposed that this newly revealed animal's scientific nomenclature be *Okapia johnstoni*; *Okapia* because he felt that it should have its own genus, since the head and teeth differed significantly from the *Helladotherium*, and *johnstoni* in honor of Johnston's contribution. It would become known by its generic name, okapi.

*   *   *

The Ituri Forest, in the northeastern corner of the Democratic Republic of Congo (Congo-Zaire), is home to the okapi and numerous other species of animals and plants. Located in the center, or heart, of Africa along the equator, it covers approximately 23,000 square miles (60,000 km²), which is about the size of the states of Connecticut, New Hampshire, and Vermont combined. The climate is quite mild, having an average temperature of 75.9°F (24.4°C). Temperatures seldom range below 70°F (21.1°C) or above 90°F (32.2°C). The Ituri experiences no drastic change of seasons although there are two distinctive rainy seasons, with April and November being the wettest months. It rains almost every day, although somewhat less rain falls in January, the driest month. The average rainfall is 78.56 inches (200 cm) and the relative humidity stays fairly constant at 95 percent. Comprising lowlands, hills, and swamps, the Ituri is very much like other rain forests of the world where the trees remain green year round. Shedding and growing new leaves continuously, a tree may have flowers and fruit at the same time. Although the soil is shallow, the nutrients are constantly being recycled. The vegetation of the forest is arranged in layers, or tiers, with certain plants and animals living within each level.

The forest is not silent. During the day, the vocalizations of birds and monkeys echo through the dense atmosphere. At night insects such as crickets and cicadas produce their characteristic sounds by rubbing their rear legs together. A tree hyrax gives its startling, screaming alarm call. Running water of meandering streams can be heard in the distance. Periodically storms stir the forest with their winds and heavy rain. The trees sway and creak, leaning upon one another in the violence. Each deluge leaves behind the smell of freshly washed nature.

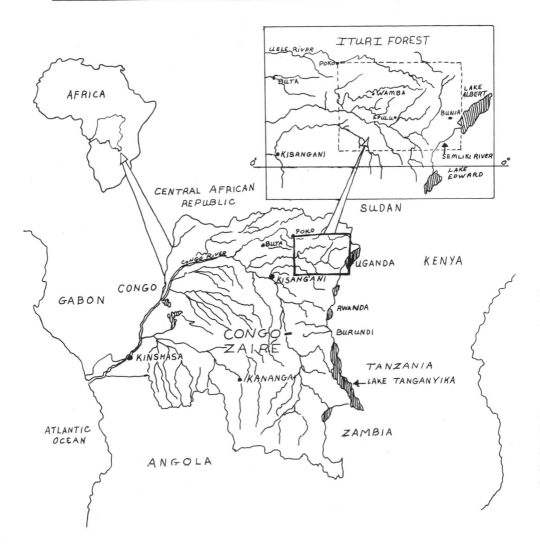

Congo-Zaire.

On quiet days, a colorful flash of a bird is glimpsed as it flits from limb to limb looking for nesting material or something tasty to eat. Slowly, a bright swallowtail butterfly flutters by in its continuing search for nectar. The young terminal leaves of some of the bushes show a reddish color against the vivid green background. Here and there, about

A forest path.

halfway up some tree trunks, epiphytes have attached themselves as shaggy, green, decorative bracelets in order to catch as much moisture and light as possible. Orchids and ferns also are attached to the trunks for support. Lying on the ground are the faded hues of petals that have fallen from blossoms high in the trees. Moss covers some of the tree trunks and buttress roots with a soft, thick, green carpet. Liana vines climb upward, leaning on the giant trees for support. Only plants that have evolved to tolerate dim sunlight can survive; these include the stout palms, lacy ferns, and delicate fungi. Grass is found only in breaks in the forest caused by fallen trees weakened by decay or storms. Only here is the sun bright and unfiltered. A few old narrow paths made centuries ago by traveling animals and humans run through the Ituri.

Every level of this rain forest has its own active, busy birds. Parrots such as the African grays, which are considered to be the best of all mimics, live here. Their ability to mimic sounds was even noted in ancient writings. African grays were kept as pets by the natives long before their discovery by Europeans. About thirteen inches (33 cm) long, this parrot appears to have an overall color of soft pastel gray except for its bright scarlet tail and black wingtips. The breast feathers have whitish margins, giving them a scalloped appearance. A bare, white facial area extends past the eyes. Seed eaters, the African grays assist in the propagation of the next generation of plants when they drop seeds onto the forest floor while feeding in the tree tops. Parrots usually travel in large flocks, making a screeching, chattering blur of color at dawn and dusk as they fly to and from their feeding areas.

African gray parrots and orchids, Disphananthe fragrantissima.

Black-billed turaco, the only green turaco in the Ituri Forest.

A black-billed turaco might be seen running along a tree limb, almost like a squirrel, foraging through the foliage for fruit and berries. The only green turaco in the Ituri, they possess unique pigments in their feathers. Bright red flight feathers contain a pigment called turacin that is about 5 percent copper and soluble in water. The vivid green they wear is also a pure pigment—the only true green pigment found in birds. Most bird coloration is due to refraction of light. The black-billed turaco's head is topped with a short, rounded crest edged in white. The bird is about sixteen inches (41 cm) in length, including its long tail.

Searching the forest floor for food, usually under fruit trees, is a rare member of the pheasant family, the Congo peacock. The quiet ways of this secretive bird made its detection difficult, and it remained unknown outside Africa until the early twentieth century. Dr. James Chapin got his first clue of its existence in 1913 when he collected only a single feather from a native's hat while traveling with Herbert Lang in the Ituri Forest in search of the okapi. Later, Chapin saw a bird mounted and incorrectly identified in a Belgian museum. On another expedition to the Congo in 1937, he was able to obtain some specimens. Pheasants are usually found only in Asia and Malaysia; this species is the only pheasant in Africa. The male is black with iridescent green, violet, and blue feathers and a crown of black and white bristle feathers on its head. A brown-and-white crown and iridescent green feathers are found on the predominantly brown, and well camouflaged, female. Although ground feeders, Congo peacocks roost in trees at night. A monogamous pair will perch on a tree limb facing one another and bow deeply while spreading their tails in a courtship display.

Fifteen primate species live in this forest; two species are nocturnal. The Angolan black-and-white colobus monkey, which is also known as the white-epauletted black colobus, lives high in the canopy and seldom comes to the ground. This agile animal's body is black except for its white, fluffy facial whiskers and shoulders covered with a shawl of long, white plumes of hair. Its tail is long, black, and ends in a large tuft of white. The colobus babies are all white at birth and gradually become darker as they age. The colobus's long, plumed shawl

Congo peacocks, Africa's only pheasant.

Angolan black-and-white colobus monkey, one of the three types of colobus monkeys found in the Ituri Forest.

was used by African tribesmen for ceremonial capes, headdresses, and shields. Legends that the colobus monkeys were messengers of the gods arose from their habit of sitting high in the treetops at sunrise and sunset as if they were in prayer. Arab traders carried their furs to Asia, where they were prized possessions. Some furs found their way to Venice. In the nineteenth century, the furs became very popular in Europe; by 1892, 175,000 skins were exported to Europe alone. Luckily, this fur went out of style—probably saving the colobus from extinction.

Chimpanzees travel the trees in the rain forest, swinging from one to another. They also move swiftly on land with a loping, three-legged gallop. A large, complex range of vocalizations and facial expressions are important in their day-to-day communication within the social groups in which they live. Some chimpanzees have been observed using tools, such as sticks, to fish termites from their mounds. Chimpanzees may also use stones to crack nuts, and where rocks are scarce they will retrieve those they used previously. Tool-use techniques and information regarding edible plants are passed on from adult to offspring.

Rain forests harbor natural wonders such as medicinal plants.

Some are discovered when observers note their use by birds and mammals. A female chimp, while suffering from an intestinal ailment, was observed to search out a rarely eaten plant, *Vernonia amugdaine,* and chew its leaves. According to the observer, she swallowed only the bitter juice. She fully recovered from her ailment, and this recovery was attributed by the observer to the medicinal properties of the ingested plant—one which natives used for a similar purpose.

Common chimpanzee.

Some facial expressions used by chimps.

Dwarf galago, or bush baby.

A nighttime arboreal feeder in the Ituri Forest is the dwarf galago, or bush baby. Smallest of all primates, it is only about eight inches (20 cm) long. Large eyes and ears and a tiny face give it an endearing expression. Its cry sounds very much like that of a human baby, hence the name "bush baby." The dwarf galago rests by day in dense foliage, hollow trees, or abandoned bird nests. During the day, it appears lethargic. At night, however, the dwarf galago is extremely active and agile as it leaps from limb to limb looking for insects, spiders, flowers, honey, fruit, or bird eggs to eat.

The largest animal residing in the Ituri is the forest elephant, a subspecies of African elephant. While about two feet (61 cm) shorter than the more-common savanna or bush elephant, the forest version has more hair and is darker in color. It carries its head lower to the ground, and its slender tusks, composed of harder ivory, closer to its

Forest elephant.

Bongo.

knees than does its savanna relatives. One easy way to identify a forest elephant is by observing its feet. It has five toenails on the forefeet and four on the hind feet, whereas the bush elephant has four on the forefeet and three on the hind feet. Like all elephant populations, their numbers have been greatly reduced by ivory poachers.

The bongo, weighing about 500 pounds (227 kg), is the largest antelope in the Ituri. Its coat is a bright chestnut red with broadly spaced, narrow white stripes that transverse its back from the shoulders to the hindquarters. Bongo horns are large, beige, and slope backward with a slight twist. Browsers, the bongo prefer the dense forest cover, especially during the hotter part of the day.

Six species of forest duikers inhabit the Ituri. Duiker (pronounced "dīker") is a Dutch word that means "dive." When alarmed, these small antelope dive into the underbrush of the forest to hide. They can also move swiftly through the forest. Because their slender forelegs are slightly shorter than their hind legs, duikers appear to stand with their backs hunched and their heads to the ground. The largest species is the yellow-backed duiker, which may stand 33 inches (84 cm) at the shoulder and weigh 100 to 140 pounds (45.4–63.5 kg). On its head is a small rufous crest, and on its back the characteristic triangular yellow stripe starts at the middle and broadens over the rump. The blue duiker, the smallest in the Ituri, weighs between 8.8 and 13.2 pounds (4–6 kg) and is slate gray in color.

The epiphytes that decorate the trees thirty to forty feet (9–12 m) above the ground may house a sleeping African tree pangolin. This unusual looking animal has large overlapping scales that cover most of its body. For this reason, it is sometimes called the scaly anteater. Although it is not related to anteaters, they do share a similar diet.

Yellow-backed duiker.

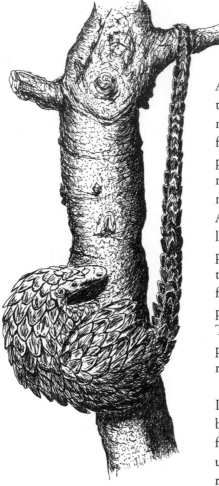

Pangolin, or scaly anteater.

A pangolin will dig into cement-hard ground termite mounds but can also break into termite tree nests by using the long claws on its forefeet while bracing with its hind legs and prehensile tail. When a cavity is made in the nest, the pangolin's sticky, wormlike tongue moves quickly to catch the escaping termites. Ants also are a preferred food item. A pangolin's enemies include man, leopards, and pythons. To escape predators it may climb the nearest tree lineman fashion, using its four feet and long muscular tail, or it may protect itself by rolling into a hard, spiky ball. The ball posture is also assumed while the pangolin sleeps high above the floor of the rain forest.

Perhaps the best-known predator in the Ituri is the leopard. Relatively small, weighing between 100 and 150 pounds (45–68 kg), this feline is strong for its size. The leopard is usually solitary and nocturnal. Its black rosettes, or rings of spots, and tawny color camouflage it well as it waits on a tree branch for prey to pass underneath. Dropping upon its chosen victim, it administers a killing bite to the neck. The leopard has the strength to nimbly climb high up into a tree while carrying captured prey, which often matches it in weight. Once its meal is treed and secured from scavengers, the cat can eat at its leisure. Nearby farmers have an unusual ally in leopards, since they prey upon

Leopard.

bushpigs and monkeys that raid crops. Leopards are strong swimmers
that love the water and often hunt prey which frequent the streams
and creeks. The feline's vocalizations, which sound like rasping coughs,
communicate territorial presence, as do clawing, rubbing their cheeks, or
spraying urine on trees. The leopard, aside from humans, is the primary
predatory threat to the okapi.

2. Description of the Okapi

Living amongst the varied wildlife of the Ituri is the okapi. Upon seeing this rare animal, one is struck by its beauty. The okapi's coat has a rich, dark brown luster with a purplish tint. Its almost deer-like face sits atop a flexible, strong, muscular neck that is relatively longer than that of other ruminants (cud chewers with four stomachs). The face is whitish gray with a black muzzle on which a few tactile hairs appear. The forehead and the centers of the large ears are a rich chestnut color that continues on the top of the head and then deepens into dark brown on the neck and back. Each okapi has a unique pattern of brown and white stripes on its legs and haunches. Often this is one's last impression of the animal as it moves gracefully and silently away.

About the size of a horse, an adult okapi stands over six feet (1.83 m) at the head and five feet (1.65 m) at the shoulder. The male can be smaller than the female in height and weight. Okapis weigh between four and seven hundred pounds (180–317 kg) and may live to over thirty years of age in captivity. They reach adult size at three but may breed earlier.

Okapi hair is short and slightly oily to the touch and has a delicate scent. Brown pigmented oil keeps the okapi's thick skin in good condition and may also serve as waterproofing in the damp rain forest of Congo-Zaire. The okapi prefers to stay dry and will take cover during a rain shower. A diurnal animal, it seeks out shade and will move out of bright sunlight to minimize heat absorption by its dark coat. Heat is dissipated through the many blood vessels on the back of an okapi's ears or via its large body surface. Adults usually appear well-groomed, with an overall sleek appearance. The calf, however, is blackish brown at birth with shaggy white stripes and a short stiff mane. The white hair that makes up the stripes is longer and softer than the brown hair. The mane is about one and a half to two inches (3.8–5.0 cm) long and sometimes extends along the spine from the back of the head to the rump. With age the calf's coat lightens, the stripes become more clear and distinct, the

Okapi foraging in the forest.

hair becomes uniform in length, and the mane disappears, leaving behind what looks like a seam running down the center of the back. The calf is probably treated as a juvenile by other okapis until the mane is lost at twelve to fourteen months of age.

The okapi's bluish gray hooves are the same color as an antelope's. However, they look more like those of the giraffe. The shape is rounded, almost circular, and slightly pointed in the front, and the hind feet are a little smaller than the forefeet. An adult footprint measures three or four inches (7.7–10.2 cm) in diameter. Each foot has two toes, making the okapi a member of the family Artiodactyla, or even-toed ungulates. The weight is distributed evenly on the flattened hooves of each foot. Scientists describe the okapi as standing on the toenails of its third and fourth digits. Traces of the second and fifth metatarsal have been found.

*Side view of okapi
calf, showing mane.*

The fore- and hind legs are about the same length and have brown and white bands around the fetlocks, which are low in the back, almost touching the ground. Brown lines run up the front of the forelegs to the knees, where there is another brown band circling the leg. Sometimes an individual will have a white dot at the knee in the center of this brown stripe, lending the appearance of a hole in a stocking. Above this are several narrow, horizontal, brown and white stripes. The hind legs are white above the fetlocks to the knee; from the knee, horizontal brown and white stripes continue up onto the haunches in a striking pattern that is different on each animal and different on the right and left sides of the same individual. This pattern of stripes has misled some who have seen the okapi for the first time into thinking that it is more closely related to the zebra than to the giraffe.

Front view of male okapi's striped legs.

The okapi's stripes help to camouflage it. In the dark forest, this animal appears to fade into the shadows. The stripes look like streaks of sunlight filtering through the trees. Even at a short distance an okapi, when it stands very still, is well camouflaged and difficult to see. The stripes also, it is believed, help the young imprint upon its mother, since the stripes are at a calf's eye level. Besides making it easy for the calf to recognize mom, they may be a "follow me" signal to the calf when the pair travel closely together. Some people believe that the stripes may also act as a stimulus during mating, as a great deal of circling, sniffing, and standing head to tail occurs at this time.

"Hole in a stocking" appearance of some okapis' knees.

"Follow me."

Unlike the giraffe, the okapi has a small gland on the front of each of its four feet where there is an infolding of the skin just above each hoof. The glands in the front feet are slightly larger than those in the hind feet. These glands are lined with hair and contain a waxy substance. There is an opening at the center where the two toes meet and through which the waxy substance may be transmitted to the bottom, middle, and back of the hoof via a small ridge along the hoof's upper surface. Although similar glands occur in some antelope and cattle, the purpose of the glands is not known. It is speculated that, in the okapi, the material contained within may provide a means of olfactory communication.

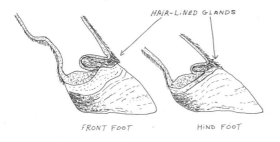

Okapi foot glands (redrawn from Pocock 1936).

As this solitary animal walks through the forest, its scented track may advertise its presence, breeding status, or even state of alarm. Perhaps this waxy substance also serves to keep the hooves in good condition.

In a manner similar to that of giraffes, okapis may use their hooves for protection. These normally placid animals may stomp the ground with their forefeet, then turn and kick with the hind feet. They can also kick out in any direction. A female will use its hooves to vigorously attack anything that gets too close to her calf. Okapis use their hooves and their speed to protect themselves from leopards and other threats. These same hooves, which carry the okapi as it crashes through the undergrowth in fear, can move noiselessly through the forest.

Walking gait of female okapi.

The tail of the okapi is brown, not striped, with a short black tuft of hair at the end reaching almost to the hocks. On occasion it is used for communication, particularly by the young. The calves will often flick their tails back and forth vigorously when excited, especially when nursing.

Head studies of female and male.

Both sexes of giraffe have horns of similar length; however, only male okapi have horns, which are four to six inches (10.2–15.3 cm) long, slope backwards at a 48 to 58 degree angle, and are covered with skin. Female okapis have whorls of hair and smaller knobs, called ossicones, where horns would be. The male okapi's horns, which are never shed, are larger than a giraffe's. As the male okapi's ossicones develop, they fuse to the frontal bones, located behind the eyes. Some researchers believe that this is a more primitive horn position than that of the giraffe. This fusion occurs when the males are between nine months and three years of age. The tips of the horns become bare of skin with time, developing a polished appearance. Competing males may use their horns in short, stabbing motions toward their opponent's flank. They may also toss their heads, thereby using their horns as a weapon. A nonreceptive female may also receive some head butts from a breeding male.

An okapi's eyes are round, large, brown, and situated laterally on the head, affording a broad field of vision. The orbits are rectangular in shape, not round as the giraffe's. When blinking, an okapi's protruding eyes appear to pull back into the sockets. Each eye has a nictitating membrane (a third eyelid that can be extended laterally across the eyeball). This membrane helps to protect the eye and keep it clean and moist. The okapi seems to have fair eyesight and some adaptation to low-light vision, including retinas with a high proportion of rods. Okapis respond readily to movement in their peripheral vision. All okapis have long, thick eyelashes. At birth a calf's eyes are surrounded by a starburst pattern of hair that makes their eyes appear larger. These eye "spots," or pseudo-eyelashes, may advertise the calf's vulnerability and will fade as the calf matures.

Calf's hair whorls and eye "spots."

In a dense rain forest, auditory (hearing) and olfactory (smell) senses may be the most important. With well-developed auditory lobes in the brain, large and flexible ears, and large auditory bullae (hollow, thin-walled bony prominences), the okapi is equipped with an enhanced ability to perceive and locate sounds. Ears edged with a short fringe of black hair and set high on the head are held stiff with cartilaginous ribs. They are readily moved individually to catch sounds.

The nostrils of the okapi are black like its muzzle. The nostril slits can be opened and closed at will. There is a distinct groove in the tissue between the nostrils in the middle of the upper lip. Referred to as the bare nasal septum, this area is moist. Tissue analysis of this area has not supported the hypothesis that it is a sensory organ. However, it might be important in capturing scent molecules for later transport to the Jacobsons organ (a specialized odor-sensing structure) located in the roof of

Okapi's independent ear movements.

the mouth. Okapis often touch their tongues to this area when investigating novel stimuli.

Males have been seen urinating on small bushes. They simultaneously cross and uncross their legs while walking across the bushes. Both males and females rub their necks on tree trunks, leaving a dark brown, oily residue. When the female is in estrus (heat, or breeding condition), it is obvious to the male by the odors and, perhaps, the sounds she emits.

The okapi's facial skull is longer than the giraffe's and provides proportionately more room for a longer tongue. Fourteen to eighteen inches (36–46 cm) in length, the tongue is pointed and bluish gray in color like the giraffe's. Okapis, considered browsers, use their prehensile tongue and mobile lips to pluck leaves from the forest understory trees. Their tongues are also used for grooming themselves and their young. They can groom their own eyes, ears, and nostrils. They may solicit mutual social grooming of areas that are difficult to reach, such as behind the ears and head. Any calf passing within the reach of its mom's active tongue will receive a lick or two. Infants are routinely seen with about an inch of their tongue protruding from their mouth for extended periods. This may be a tactile (touch), gustatory (taste), and olfactory means of sampling their environment.

*Okapi named
Kwanini, browsing.*

Mother grooms calf with her long tongue.

Calf's tongue protrudes while investigating its surroundings.

Based on the animal's outward appearance, the first explorers to see an okapi thought it was a type of zebra. But when the skulls of the okapi and the giraffe were compared, it became clear that they were more closely related. The okapi's skull lies on a lower, flatter plane than the giraffe's, which may indicate that it represents an older and more primitive branch of the family Giraffidae. A young okapi's face is almost square. As the skull grows, its length increases more rapidly than its width, giving the face a more slender appearance. The sutures of the cerebral skull usually close between the juvenile and subadult stages; however, the facial sutures close later. There appears to be no sexual difference in okapi skulls other than the presence of horns in the male. The brain mass to body mass ratio is larger in the okapi than it is in the giraffe. Scientists differ on the significance of this discrepancy in size, but some believe this would indicate that the okapi is more intelligent.

The okapi's dentition is of the same type and arrangement as the giraffe's. There are a total of thirty-two teeth, which appear wrinkled or

Skulls of okapi and giraffe
(redrawn from Lankester 1902b).

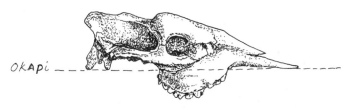

OKAPI

SKULLS SHOWN AT THE SAME AGE.

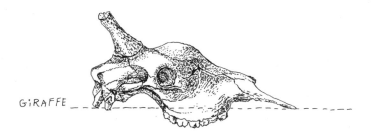

GIRAFFE

Female eats the top of a broken sapling.

rugose. The dental formula is o/o/3/3 (incisor/canine/premolar/molar) in the upper jaw and 3/1/3/3 in the lower jaw. Both sides of the upper jaw have neither incisors nor canine teeth but only a callous pad where these teeth would be. There are three premolars and three molars on each side. The lower jaw contains three incisors, one canine, three premolars, and three molars on each side. The canines have a lobed (rounded) appearance that is distinctive to the giraffe family. However, the okapi's canines are two-lobed, while the giraffe's may have three or four lobes. Premolars and molars have low crowns for grinding. By the time the calf reaches seven weeks of age, the milk teeth, or deciduous dentures, have nearly erupted. The upper teeth come in before the lower teeth; the lower canines erupt last. The large gap between the front teeth and the premolars in the upper jaw makes it possible for the okapi to strip leaves from branches. It is also helpful for bending saplings over so that the top leaves can be reached. Delicately using the callous pad in the upper jaw and the incisors in the lower jaw with its muscular tongue, the okapi can pick the most tender leaves from the trees overhead.

Male okapi's elongated neck and sloping back.

Skeletal similarities also are indicative of the close relationship between the giraffe and the okapi. Most notably this includes the slightly elongated neck and sloping back. This slope may help balance the longer, muscular neck. Okapi vertebrae are not as long as those of the giraffe; but they are more massive than those of other ruminants. The spinal column consists of seven cervical, fourteen thoracic (each with a pair of ribs), five lumbar, and four or five sacral vertebrae. In contrast, the cervical vertebrae of the giraffe are elongated and it possesses only three or four sacral vertebrae.

The larynx of okapis and giraffes are simple, having only rudimentary vocal cords. Long thought of as a quiet animal, the okapi has a humanly audible repertoire that consists of chuffs (or cough calls), moans (emitted by males during courtship), snorts, whistles or bellows (when in acute distress), and bleats (emitted by the calves). Recently it was discovered

Female "chuffs" to another okapi.

that the okapi is capable of producing and receiving very low frequency sounds (infrasonic). The source of these sounds, many of which are below the range of human hearing, is hard to locate. This may afford the animal protection from predators while allowing for communication with conspecifics (other members of this species). Infrasonic calls also carry well through dense vegetation and warm, moist air. Elephants and rhinoceros also are known to produce infrasonic vocalizations. Large sinus areas are thought necessary to produce infrasonic sounds. The okapi, giraffe, elephant, and rhinoceros all possess such structures.

Other internal organs of the head, neck, and chest of the okapi, including salivary glands, thyroid, thymus, tonsils, and lungs, are similar to those of other ruminants. They all have a two-lobed left lung and a right lung with four lobes. The respiration rate of an immobilized

Equipped for infrasonic communication.

(sedated) adult okapi ranges between sixteen and twenty-four breaths per minute, and that of a calf ranges between thirty-six and forty-two per minute.

The okapi's heart makes up 0.4 percent of its body weight and is four chambered, as with all mammals. The average heart rate ranges between 88 and 136 beats per minute for an adult and between 100 and 112 for a calf. A comparison of the blood protein serum and globulin

Male okapi chewing cud.

of the giraffe and the okapi shows their close affinity. Okapis have extremely low cholesterol values.

Like cows, the okapi and giraffe swallow food partially chewed and later regurgitate a cud (a bolus or mass) which is then chewed more thoroughly before being reswallowed. The first stomach, or rumen, is where the cellulose of the leaves is broken down by bacteria. Food then passes into the reticulum, where fermentation occurs and boluses are formed for regurgitation and rechewing. The contraction of stomach muscles, which forces the bolus up the esophagus to the mouth, can be easily observed. Once in the mouth, the bolus is mixed with saliva while being rechewed. When the mass is reswallowed, it enters the omasum, where folds absorb the alkaline fluid. From the omasum, the less-diluted food mass passes into the abomasum. Here it is mixed with gastric juices before entering the intestines to be broken down into nutrients easily absorbed into the bloodstream. The residue enters the large intestines, where water reabsorption occurs. Okapis have large cecums and colons that assist in microbial digestion of food. An appendix is present, but neither giraffes nor okapis have gall bladders.

*Calf named Makasi,
reclining.*

Okapi feces are rounded pellets of about one inch (2.5 cm) in diameter. Okapis often defecate repeatedly in the same place. Called focal
excretion, this may be one method an animal uses to mark its territory
or home range. The shape of the pellets is often individualistic. In fact,
animals being tracked in the wild have been identified by these "calling
cards." Reflective of their browsing diet, adult okapi urine is normally
alkaline (8.0–9.0 pH). Urine is sometimes sampled by the individual
producing it or by another okapi. Males can ascertain a female's reproductive status by this method.

*   *   *

So much of what we know about this animal has only recently been
revealed through scientific study of the captive population. In many
ways, the okapi remains an animal of mystery. Following its discovery by
Europeans, there would continue to be much speculation regarding its
taxonomic origins.

On May 7, 1901, when the Zoological Society of London displayed the two okapi skulls and the skin that had been sent to them by Sir Harry Johnston, the following appeared in *The Times*:

A NEW MAMMAL

The Helladotherian is alive in the Congo Free-State. This remarkable creature in fact appears as far as a cursory examination of its skin and skull may guide us, to be a living representative of the Helladotherium, a creature found in the fossil state in Greece and Asia Minor and supposed to be extinct . . .

Male okapi with ears alert.

Helladotherium was an early giraffe, and in the final assessment the new animal would be included in that family. Johnston, at the June 8, 1901, meeting of the society would suggest the scientific name *Helladotherium tigrunum*. After much study, Sir E. Ray Lankester would suggest later that year that the animal be named *Okapia johnstoni*.

In 1902 a Belgian officer, Lieutenant Leoni, sent two skins and a skeleton from the Congo to Brussels for study. The scientist who received them asked a British authority on fossil mammals, Dr. Forsyth Major, to come and examine these new acquisitions. Dr. Major concluded that they represented a different species of okapi, and he named it *Okapia liebrechti*. In 1903, Lord Rothschild obtained another skin of an okapi. Dr. Lankester examined it and determined that it was yet another species of okapi, which he named *Okapia erikssoni*. This was in honor of Lieutenant Eriksson, who had sent Sir Harry Johnston the first okapi skin and skulls in 1901 and who Johnston hoped would receive credit for his role in the discovery. According to experts, there were now three species of okapis. However, the experts soon realized that only one species of okapi actually existed. Differences in the specimens were actually attributable to sex, age, individual variations, and the manner in which the natives prepared the skins. The genital organs

Female okapi with longer, more slender neck.

Ancestor—pronghorn, deer, or cow?

were always cut away, which made it impossible to ascertain the sex of each specimen.

Some controversy persists among scientists as to the common ancestry of the giraffe family, including the okapi. There are three theories. First, that the ancient animal had a cow or antelope like ancestor (family Bovidae). Second, that it had a deer-like ancestor (Cervidae), and third, that its ancestors were pronghorn-like (Antilocapridae). Since the pronghorn evolved strictly in the New World, it seems highly unlikely that it is the ancestor of an animal that evolved in Europe, Asia, and Africa. The fact that both cattle and giraffe possess permanent horns lent credence to the belief that giraffes evolved from Bovidae. However, most zoologists believe that the giraffids were derived from Cervidae (deer). This assumption is based mainly on characteristics of the teeth. The horns of the giraffe and okapi also resemble deer antlers "in velvet." The giraffe and okapi do not shed their horns as most Cervidae do, and their horns usually remain at least partially covered with skin throughout their lives.

A second controversy arises concerning the place of origin of the giraffids. Most paleontologists believe that they evolved in Europe and

Asia and then migrated into Africa. Others, however, believe that their origin was in Africa and they then spread outward from that source.

The earliest giraffe probably evolved about twenty-five million years ago in North Africa. One of these was *Prolibytherium magnieri,* which had two large, flattened, fan-shaped horns which were permanently covered with skin. These horns were never discarded.

Prolibytherium magnieri.

Paleotraginae (subfamily), classified as the first true giraffe, appeared about ten million years ago and disappeared two million years ago. It was a medium-sized animal with a slightly elongated neck and legs. Two forehead structures and a pair of head horns covered with skin made it look very much like the okapi. However, scientists

doubt that the okapi is simply a slightly
different, direct descendant of this
giraffid and have placed the okapi in
a subfamily of its own, Okapiinae.

    Another evolutionary line of
giraffe was the subfamily Sivatheriinae,
to which the genus *Helladotherium*
belonged. These were stout, sturdy
animals, moose-like in appearance and
about the size of elephants. They had
huge, odd-shaped, skin-covered horns.
At one time, Sivatherium were wide-
spread throughout North Africa,
Europe, and Asia. They died out about
5,000 years ago. Their likeness appears
in Sumerian (Iraqi) art from around
this period. Some believe that they can
see the images of these early giraffids
in the central Saharan neolithic
petroglyphs, or rock carvings,
dating from perhaps
8,000 years ago.

Paleotraginae.

Sivatheriinae.

According to some Egyptologists, certain representations of the god Seth-Typhon resemble an okapi or giraffe.

In modern times there are only two genera of giraffe and one species within each; *Giraffa camelopardalis* and *Okapia johnstoni*, the giraffe and the okapi. One species evolved long legs to run on the

Size comparison between giraffe and okapi.

African plains and a long neck to reach food in the sub-Saharan savanna and woodland tree tops where no other animal could feed. The other retreated to a dense rain forest habitat of central Africa where its coloration and behavioral traits would offer it protection and in which there were plenty of fresh green leaves to eat with little competition. Yet both species retain features that indicate their descent from ancient giraffids.

There has been much speculation on how the giraffe came by its scientific name, *Giraffa camelopardalis*. One theory is that the genus name *Giraffa* may come from the Arabic word *zurafah,* which has several meanings including "creature of grace," "one who walks swiftly," and "tallest of all mammals." Another theory cites that in 1022 an Arab geographer wrote that the father of the giraffe was a leopard and the mother was a camel. Hence the species name *camelopardalis* reflected this theory, which was supposed to explain how an animal with spots could look and walk like a camel. Most ungulates use an alternating leg movement, as depicted by the familiar trot of a horse. An animal exhibiting alternate walk will move the right front leg forward with the left hind leg, then as the left front leg moves forward so does the right hind leg.

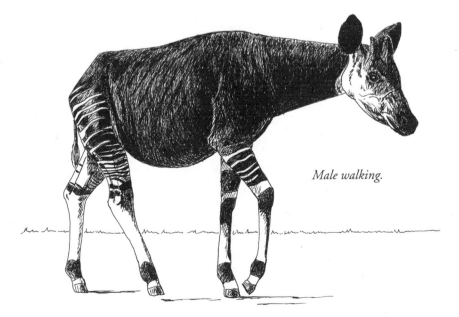

Male walking.

The okapi has two main gaits of locomotion, an ambling walk called "pacing" and a gallop. When pacing at about ten miles an hour (16 kph), the foreleg and the hind leg on one side of the body move forward simultaneously, followed by the legs on the other side. The animal's weight is supported by both legs on one side and then by both legs on the other side; this is called lateral leg movement. The okapi's relatively longer neck may be helpful in coordinating its pacing gait.

Some scientists believe that diagonal or alternate leg use is a more primitive method of locomotion than lateral leg movement. It is seen in amphibians, reptiles, and early quadrupeds (four legged animals). This means of walking may afford better balance. Although an animal that uses lateral leg movement may sacrifice some stability, the longer stride may provide a speed advantage, as evidenced by the fact that pacing horses move faster than trotters. Also, the body and leg muscles may work together more efficiently, and it is impossible for the hind leg to inadvertently hit the front leg.

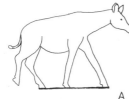

A

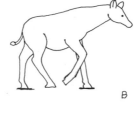

B

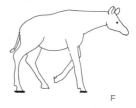

C

D

E

F

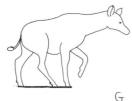

G

H

Sketch of okapi's pacing gait.

An okapi can gallop at thirty-five miles an hour (56.3 kph) while maintaining the basic right-side then left-side leg movement. However, there seems to be a slight movement of the head and neck at a gallop. When startled, a stationary okapi will push off with both hind legs, thereby attaining speed more quickly.

To settle itself on the ground, an okapi will bend its forelegs and go down on its knees. The head will be stretched forward as the animal bends its hind legs underneath. As the animal settles, the head will again rise to an upright position.

Female named Goma, reclining.

When a resting okapi attempts to get up, its weight and head will swing forward as it places its rear hooves solidly underneath its body. The weight is shifted to the rear as the animal rests on its knees, and then the forelegs are extended. This movement results in the okapi standing on all four feet.

* * *

Research on captive okapis descended from the original founder stock has greatly enhanced our knowledge of this species. However, procurement of healthy specimens for the world's zoos would prove to be a difficult and arduous task.

3. Captivity

After the May 7, 1901, exhibit of the two skulls and the skin sent from Uganda, the competition to attain a complete specimen of an okapi for display began. Of course the greatest accomplishment would be to bring the first live animal out of the "dark continent" and to exhibit it in the increasingly popular zoological gardens.

In 1902 within the Ituri District of the Congo, Commandant Sillye, a Belgian officer, sent one of his lieutenants to obtain more specimens for the Belgian government. Lieutenant Anzelius returned with six skins and the dubious honor of being the first European to kill an okapi. Commandant Sillye captured the first live okapi in 1903—a young animal that soon escaped.

So many expeditions from leading museums were sent in an attempt to secure a specimen that the Belgian government imposed a ban on hunting okapis without a special permit. The Congo Expedition, sponsored by the American Museum of Natural History and the New York

Calf exploring.

Zoological Society, departed from New York City in May 1909 with plans for a five-year collecting tour. These prominent institutions had obtained all the necessary permits from the Belgian government. The venture was headed by Herbert Lang, a mammalogist, accompanied by an eighteen-year-old ornithologist, James P. Chapin, who would discover the Congo peacock in 1937. With them, they carried a list of animals that the society wanted to capture alive for exhibit. Included on this list was the now famous okapi and the white rhinoceros. The expedition would return to New York in November of 1915—nearly six and a half years later—with 55 tons of collected materials, including 10,000 photographs, 4,000 ethnological objects (cultural artifacts), 5,800 mammals, 6,200 birds, 4,800 reptiles, 6,000 fish, and more than 100,000 invertebrates, plus volumes of letters and field notes.

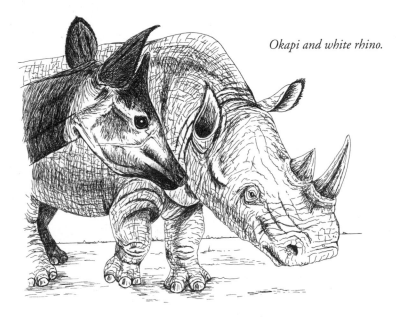

Okapi and white rhino.

After traveling up the Congo River twelve hundred miles and walking inland for twenty-one days, the expedition one evening came upon a village that was drying okapi meat over a fire. At last they knew they were in okapi country. So prized was the skin of the okapi among the Bantu farmers that the privilege of sitting upon it was reserved for the chieftain and his family. One limb of the hide could purchase a wife. Many superstitions surrounded the okapi. Wearing a portion of the skin was purported to endow the wearer with the cunning of an okapi to elude its enemies. To kill an okapi improperly could bring many curses upon the reckless offender.

Lang was traveling with only twenty porters, but the natives were suspicious of the twelve Belgian soldiers who accompanied the explorers under the dictates of governmental regulations. Lang, realizing that he would not otherwise get the natives' assistance in capturing an okapi, sent the soldiers back to the nearest garrison. This was a brave gesture, since Westerners reported that cannibalism still occurred in this area. Only six years earlier, fighting had erupted between the natives and Belgian soldiers. Thornton, an American in Belgian service, and fifty of his soldiers and porters were reported as killed and eaten. Cannibalism was "officially" abolished in the region after three years of fighting.

Every day, as Lang and Chapin worked in the village, natives came to see "Banda's white men" (white men from Banda territory). The natives would wait for hours just to shake their hands. They would stroke both men's arms and say, "Nyama mingi! Nyama nzuri!" Translated, this phrase means "lots of meat, very good meat." Lang thought that they were popular with the natives because of their personalities and as curiosities until he heard the translation, which sent cold chills down his spine. The natives laughingly added that they would not kill the white men, because they would have to send all the meat to the chiefs. Reportedly, white men were considered a delicacy because they ate lots of salt, which made them tastier.

In the *New York Zoological Society Bulletin* of May 1918, Lang wrote:

After many lengthy palavers I finally succeeded in overcoming their superstitions. I soon had stationed in their camps in the forest our native assistants, and finally, as news of the Okapi arrived, I ran out day by day crossing swamps and rivers as they themselves did, slept in the forest, and joined their hunting parties even in the dead of night. I had but two porters with me, one for my camera and the other for my necessary camp outfit, an equipment so meager that a Belgian officer laughingly called it 'the tablet-form outfit'. This gave us a reputation with the natives and our absolute fairness with them secured their confidence.

He added, "Those who can rightfully claim to have seen a living Okapi, or shot one, have been so favored quite accidentally." Lang would soon be so blessed.

It had rained all night and droplet showers fell from the leaves onto the small group as they passed through the forest. Lang and his guide, Amadu, had walked ten miles when they picked up the tracks of two okapis traveling together. The two men followed the tracks late into the afternoon to where the okapis had parted. They knew they were very near one of the animals. For an hour they crept through the heavy vegetation until they were within fifteen feet. Suddenly they heard the swish of a tail and the stamp of a foot. The animal bolted away through the thick vegetation. This was as close as Lang had yet come to seeing a live okapi.

A powerful Azande chief, Akenge, had already been of great help to Lang by making contributions to the expedition's collection. He promised to provide Lang with a young okapi. Six weeks later Lang was informed that the chief's son, Abawe, was to capture the okapi calf.

On the fifth night after Abawe arrived in camp, one of his messengers announced to Lang, "The young Okapi will be caught tomorrow." Abawe left early in the morning, eating nothing, touching nothing that would diminish the mystical charm with which he had surrounded himself. It was a clear day and around noon when Lang's party arrived at the appointed place. Abawe appeared and instructed two of his men to take circular paths down the hill to a brook that the okapis drank from and crossed daily. Within thirty minutes, one of the men returned, stating that the okapis had not yet crossed the stream.

Abawe was certain that the okapis were still on the hill. He walked cautiously for about a hundred yards (91 m). There was a loud crash as the mother fled, but the calf was not at her side.

Looking around, the men found small tracks that led to a diminutive version of mom hiding in the bushes. Lang described the following scene as Abawe picked up the calf:

> Holding the calf in his arms as firmly as if it were a struggling lion, he called desperately for lianas with which to bind it. All hands were ready, for that was big game! But everyone had to laugh. The terrible beast had no other desire than to lick the face of its captor and to suck the fingers

held out to him. It was as tame as a lamb and enjoyed being patted and stroked. Abawe thought it had been bewitched so he would receive no presents from the white man for catching a thing tamer than any goat. All cheered him and a dance was held on the very spot, during which the young Okapi peacefully settled in the shade.

Lang fed the calf condensed milk, but his supply ran out within four days. Although he sent for more, none was available. He tried a mixture of rice and water, but the calf became increasingly weaker. After ten days Lang gave up all hope of saving it. This sad occurrence made him realize how difficult it would have been to transport this animal from the center of Africa.

Lang's calf.

To the great chief, Akenge, Lang sent pipes, tobacco, salt, matches, perfume, and soap. In return Akenge sent Lang a token of his friendship. The gift consisted of two magic whistles carved from wood and decorated with polished iron rings. Lang was to choose which one he wanted. To own one was to have all your enemies killed. To own the other was to make many friends. Lang chose the latter.

For many years attempts to export a living okapi from Africa failed. The capture and transport of the okapi was arduous. Early capture attempts usually involved a pit several feet deep placed along known trails. The hole was covered with sticks and branches and, finally, with leaves. When the okapi walked onto the pit cover, the fragile braces gave way and the animal crashed to the bottom while branches and leaves fell all around it.

The frightened animal could not escape. The scent of humans was detectable, and loud, shouting human voices approached. Natives would push and guide the okapi into the even smaller space of a shipping crate. Placed on a truck, the crated animal would travel the rough jungle roads for hundreds of miles to the Zaire (Congo) River.

During the trip, which lasted several days, the animal would be jostled and shaken. If the crate was not padded, the okapi could receive abrasions or more severe injuries. The mesh screen over the crate afforded little protection against the biting and stinging insects that assaulted the captive. While investigating the screen, the animal might tear and ingest some of the material, which could lead to digestive trouble or even death.

During land transport and the approximately three week boat ride to the capital of Kinshasa, the food offered to the captive was rarely appropriate for a browser. Lack of proper nutrition caused a decline in appetite and general health, as did the fact that the crated okapi was forced to stand in urine and feces accumulated since its capture. The slick wet floor would sometimes cause the animal to slide, lose its balance, and fall. Upon reaching the capital city, the okapi might have been put in an enclosure with fresh food while it waited for train transport to a port city where a steamer to Europe or America awaited. Most often, it was left standing in its dirty shipping crate until placed on a railroad car with some food that would soon spoil. At the dock, it would probably wait several days, perhaps in the sun, before being placed on the steamer. This last leg of the voyage lasted many weeks. All fodder on board would soon become uneatable. Seasickness might result in refusal to eat. The okapi would become weak, unable to rise, and then die.

If the captive okapi survived the several-week-long ocean voyage, a lengthy quarantine and inexperienced caregivers awaited. The ninety-day quarantine involved immobilizing the okapi at least three times for blood tests. Eventually, the inception of airplanes and increased knowledge about the species made it a little easier to get the okapi out of Africa. The trip, however, would still involve long truck rides over rough African

terrain and changing planes two
or three times. To this day, it is not
easy to move an okapi from its home
into captivity. Additionally, endless
paper work has always been required
by the countries involved.

    The first-recorded successful
hand-rearing of an okapi calf is
attributed to Mrs. Landeghem, wife
of the district commissioner of Buta
in the Uele District of the Congo.
She used a mixture of condensed and
fresh cow's milk to feed the female
calf, which she called Buta. This calf
was also the first okapi successfully
exported out of Africa to a European
zoo. Arriving at the Antwerp Zoo
in August, 1919, Buta also had the
distinction of being the first okapi
to be seen outside her native country.
Unfortunately she would survive
only seven weeks. Another female,
Tele, exported in 1928, was the first
to survive for any length of time. She
lived at the Antwerp Zoo until 1943,
when she died of starvation during
World War II.

Kiyowe as a calf.

    From 1927 until 1941, the only shipping station for okapis was oper-
ated by a Belgian Catholic missionary, Brother Joseph Hutsebaut, who
seemed to have a way with the animals. He helped capture and raise
fifteen okapis in the village of Buta. His knowledge made it possible for
the successful transport of okapis to Antwerp, London, and New York.

    In 1934 Commander Attilio Gatti was sent by the London Zoo to
capture a live okapi. Although he would eventually capture two animals,
his attempt to use chloroform to capture and transport an okapi failed.
The chloroform had a marked effect on the people handling the liquid
but failed to produce a response in the animal. He related another

incident when an okapi was caught in a pit around which a fence had been constructed. A rope was placed around the animal's neck in order to encourage it to walk up a ramp adjacent to the pit. However, the male okapi broke free of the enclosure and ran off into nearby water with the rope dangling behind. The animal was recaptured by securing the rope to a tree, but then a violent thunderstorm suddenly developed. Afraid that the okapi might die of fright while the men were attempting to load it on a stretcher, Gatti released it.

Other early attempts also met failure. In one case, a mother was chased off by hunters' duplicating the noise of a falling tree, but the captured calf died fifteen days later. Another method involved driving the okapi out of the pit into a bottomless transport box. The box was then lifted slightly from the ground and carried through the forest. The okapi was forced to walk along with the box, resulting in numerous abrasions.

Due to Brother Hutsebaut's skill with okapis, the Belgian colonial regime approached him about a formal position to capture okapis for export. He responded that he had come to the Congo to preach the Word of God, not to catch okapis. The job was given to Patrick Putnam, an American anthropologist.

Where the slow, wide Epulu River becomes narrow and fast, Camp Putnam, or Epulu, was founded in 1928. While passing through this area, Patrick Putnam had decided to stay and build his home there. Epulu became an organized capture station under the direction of Jean de Medina from 1948 through most of the 1960s. Jean Bosco would be in charge until 1987 when a Swiss couple, Rosemarie and Karl Ruf, took over. Between 1947 and 1990, sixty-six animals were sent to European and American zoos. The percentage of exported okapis to survive more than one year in captivity remained low until recent years. In addition, many animals died during capture, at holding stations, or during transport.

The strain of the trip and adapting to new surroundings took their toll on imported okapis. Stress gave internal parasites an unfair advantage, and the health of the okapi often declined dangerously during transport. During the move, they could become infected with trypanosomes, a blood parasite. Intestinal and liver worms caused the most problems. These parasites laid large numbers of eggs, which were excreted in the host's feces. During transport, animals in shipping crates were in constant contact with their own infested feces. This problem was accentuated by the sealing of the crates to prevent the possibility of spreading African parasites and diseases to the destination country. In the early years, okapis that survived their voyages to zoos often died of parasitic infections. In 1935 London received its first okapi. A gift from Prince Leopold to the Duke of Windsor, this adult died within four months from a parasitic infection. Two years later, King George VI of England was offered another okapi. After officials examined the droppings of available okapis with a microscope, the animal with the least parasites was chosen. This male, who was named Buta, lived at the London Zoo for almost thirteen years before dying of pneumonia.

Over thirty species of worms can be found in okapis; many can be controlled with medication. The most dangerous parasite is the nematode *Monodontella giraffea,* which affects the bile ducts and liver. Okapis are

Mother inspecting newborn.

also very susceptible to bacterial infections. Meticulous cleanliness is very important in keeping this animal healthy. A lack of understanding of this principle contributed to some of the early losses in captivity.

In recent years, okapis held at Epulu have been treated prior to transport to reduce their parasitic load, thereby resulting in a higher rate of survival after shipment. Air transport also has helped to decrease losses. In 1948 the first okapi to travel by plane was flown to Copenhagen. Currently, only offspring born and raised in captivity at Epulu are exported to zoos and breeding centers. These animals seem not to be as stressed by captivity and adapt more easily to transfers.

Propagation in zoos was also hampered by our lack of knowledge about this species. Until recent years, almost half of the calves born in captivity would not survive to reach their second birthday.

The first European birth occurred at the Antwerp Zoo in 1954; however, the male calf, named Hoka, did not survive. Its father, Besobe, arrived in Antwerp in 1948 and its mother, Dasegela, in 1950. Three subsequent offspring also would die; the first as a result of maternal aggression. Removing the other two calves from the mother would prolong their lives; however, only one would survive for more than a few weeks.

Ebola was born in Paris on June 6, 1957, and would live there for twenty-two years (until August 26, 1979). She was the first okapi calf to be successfully conceived, born, and mother-reared in captivity.

The first okapi in North America *"Malaika."* was Congo, a two-year-old male that arrived at the Bronx Zoo on August 3, 1937. Congo had been bottle-reared by Brother Hutsebaut at Buta. W. Reid Blair, director of the New York Zoological Park, selected this okapi from among three males that had recently arrived at the Antwerp Zoo because he was relatively free of parasites. In 1949 arrangements were made to obtain a mate for Congo. Unfortunately no one checked the sex of the animal prior to shipment, and upon arrival it was noted that the new okapi, Bilota, had a nice set of horns. Congo would die in 1952 without a mate. On November 1, 1956, a female, Muyoni, arrived as a state gift from the Belgian Congo. Together Bilota and Muyoni produced four male calves, three of which lived past six years of age. Their first calf, Nejoma, was born on October 17, 1959. He missed being the first calf born in the United States by only one month. That milestone would be claimed by Mr. G, who was born at the Chicago Zoological Park (Brookfield) on September 17, 1959. In 1960 and 1961, Mr. G also had the distinction of being exhibited by a circus (Ringling Bros. and Barnum and Bailey).

Calf and mother.

Other zoos would claim their first okapi births over the next four years. Rotterdam's first, a female named Ituri, was born February 12, 1960. Henri was born at Basel on February 28, 1960. Frankfurt produced its first calf, Kiwu, on September 9, 1960. On June 17, 1961, Tove, a female, was born at the Copenhagen Zoo, and on February 8, 1962, Baruti was born at the San Diego Zoo. On November 23, 1963, the first okapi born in England, Zamba, was born at the Bristol Zoo. Zoo officials watched the birth on closed-circuit television. Unfortunately, the calf soon died as the result of a fungal infection from the barn hay. The first okapi born at the Dallas Zoo, Sibiti, arrived on November 28, 1963.

Four sets of twins have been born in captivity; all were premature (normal gestation period is 14.5 months) and none survived. In 1976 the Bristol Zoo had a pair of females. In Paris, okapi parents Pablo and Pastourelle had two sets of male twins, one set in 1981 and another in 1984. Male and female twins were aborted at four or five months in London in 1985.

Two unsuccessful caesarean deliveries were performed in Bristol in 1979. Neither the calves nor the mothers survived. More recent attempts to deliver okapis by caesarean section at Bristol and London zoos also have failed.

A few okapis have lived unusually long lives. The Paris Zoo can boast of a wild-caught male that lived in captivity for thirty-three years. A captive-born male lived thirty years in Paris. Both Brookfield (in Chicago) and Madrid, Spain, have had females that lived almost thirty years. A wild-caught female at Rotterdam died at approximately thirty-one years of age. The Dallas Zoo's Sibiti was almost thirty-one years old when she died in 1994 at the Brookfield Zoo.

The captive population in Europe descends from twenty-three okapis, while the North American stock has twenty-five founders. The majority of these animals were removed from a very localized area, increasing the likelihood of relatedness and some lack of genetic variability from the start. Very few animals are being removed from the wild—only four since 1984—and then only when it is necessary to bring in new genes for the benefit of all okapis. It is estimated that there are only between 10,000 and 20,000 okapis remaining in Congo-Zaire. They are distributed over a large area centered on the Ituri Forest. This species is dramatically affected by habitat change and human pressures. The small captive-born population is thus even more precious.

*   *   *

Quality captive care hinges upon animal care personnel who are knowledgeable about the physiology and behavior of this unique animal, both as a species and as individuals. Okapis are flighty, so caregivers need to be steady, calm, and reasonably quiet as they go about their duties.

Jumping okapi calf.

Eventually they become familiar with each animal's likes and dislikes with regard to food, situations, and other relevant information that comes from working daily with them. Keepers can often predict how an individual animal will respond to being introduced to other animals. When a new calf is born, experienced keepers know generally what to anticipate, and they keep a watchful eye for anything of concern (such as excessive perineal grooming, aggression by the mother toward her new offspring, or an ailing calf).

Normally a solitary animal, the okapi does not seem to mind being separated from other animals. At night, or during inclement weather, each animal is often placed alone in a stall. This arrangement allows the keeper to easily monitor an individual's diet. The keepers visually check each animal in the morning to be certain that they have not injured themselves or developed observable health problems overnight. Throughout the day, each animal will be periodically checked. If concerns arise, appropriate supervisory and medical personnel are notified.

Of primary importance in captive care is cleanliness. To prevent the development of a parasitic problem, the living quarters must be kept clean. Each day the stalls are cleaned, old bedding (hay or wood shavings) removed, the floors washed, and new bedding put down. Stalls are disinfected on a regular basis (once a week), but if an individual develops a problem it may be done more frequently. Stalls are large with access to an outside holding area or exhibit. Feces and any object that might harm the okapi are removed from outside yards or exhibits.

Captive okapis prefer to walk on familiar and well-worn paths, just as their wild counterparts do, often stopping to investigate any new or interesting object. This characteristic can be used to obtain periodic weights. By placing a walk-on platform scale in transfer areas between the stall and outside area, keepers can easily monitor the weight of their charges. The okapi will often stop on the scale to investigate a strategically placed, favored browse item. Weights are useful as gauges of normal growth patterns and health, and for monitoring pregnancies.

Modern caregivers attempt to provide an opportunity for captive okapis to display a full repertoire of natural behaviors. Okapis in the wild spend a majority of their time foraging from over two hundred species of plants, but the majority of their food comes from only thirty species.

Young male reaching for browse.

A captive okapi is encouraged to explore its surroundings and to use its tongue. Browse may be placed within easy reach of the okapi or at a height that necessitates the animal's stretching its limber neck and long gray tongue. Many exhibits are planted with suitable browse (bamboo, hackberry, willow), and any leaves within reach are soon consumed. Fresh produce—such as pieces of carrots, apples, onions, and other fruits and vegetables—is often placed on the animal's feed or on the branches of "treat trees" hung in its stall. Produce and browse provide additional moisture and fiber to the okapi's diet.

The primary staples of a captive okapi's diet are a nutritionally complete pelleted feed and alfalfa hay. A measured quantity of a specially prepared pelleted feed (17 percent crude protein, 16 percent acid detergent fiber) is presented to each animal daily. Although

Captive okapi drinking.

smaller, males normally receive a larger amount than females. Lactating females receive the most feed in order to help them meet the nutritional requirements of their calves. Alfalfa is usually provided in seemingly limitless supply (*ad libitum*). It must be of high quality (17–24 percent crude protein, 21–40 percent acid detergent fiber), not be too dry, and have a high ratio of leaves to stems. Hay that is too dry often causes problems with mouth abscesses and more frequent drinking. Some animals will drop dry alfalfa into water, allowing it to soak prior to eating it.

Fresh water is always accessible. Although okapis usually drink infrequently, they may drink copious amounts at one time. Little is known of their drinking behavior in the wild. It is believed that okapi obtain most of their water from their browse.

Some facilities may also offer oatmeal daily. It is used to administer medication to the animals when necessary or as a reinforcer for desired behaviors. Small portions of fruits and vegetables—such as endive, lettuce, spinach, apples, carrots, onion, bananas, pears, and strawberries—may be offered during the day. In all, captive okapi may eat ten to sixteen pounds (4.5–7.3 kg) of food a day.

Mineral or salt blocks (without selenium) are placed in the stalls at most facilities. Okapis may consume about one and a half to two ounces (50 to 60 gm) per day. In the wild, they have been seen licking a lightly salty, sulphurous, reddish clay from along rivers, charcoal from trees hit by lightning, and bat guano deposits in hollow trees—perhaps as a means of obtaining needed minerals.

Okapis reach adult size at approximately three years; however, they are capable of reproduction at an earlier age. The onset of puberty in okapis has been reported as two to four years for males and one and a half to three years for females. In captivity the youngest female to conceive was one year and seven months old, while the youngest male to breed was two years and two months old. When natural breeding might first begin in the wild is unknown.

While most captive male okapis start breeding approximately one year later than females, they continue to sire healthy calves for a longer period. An initial decline in fertility is seen only at age twenty-four for males, and in captivity a thirty-three-year-old sired a viable calf. Production of healthy calves declines rapidly once a female reaches the

Okapi spreading its front legs so its head can reach the ground.

age of fifteen to seventeen, although a female can continue to calve up to the age of twenty-six. This type of information is not available for the wild population.

Most mature, captive female okapis experience estrus every fourteen to fifteen days year-round with no evidence of seasonality. However, some females may experience irregular cycling or time periods when no cycles occur.

Much is still to be learned regarding the endocrinology of this unique animal. Both estrogen and progesterone metabolites are present in the urine and feces of female okapis. The estrous cycle can be inferred and pregnancy confirmed by analyzing urine for the presence and relative concentrations of pregnanediol-3-glucuronide, a progesterone metabolite. Females can be conditioned to wait for a food reward before first urination in the morning. Using urinalysis and observations of reproductive behavior, birth dates can be predicted. Urinalysis is also used to determine the onset of regular cycling after delivery. The concentration of progesterone metabolites is actually higher in feces than in urine, and a recently developed assay can delineate the estrous cycle from fecal samples. However, neither the urine nor fecal assays are completely reliable. Absolute confirmation of pregnancy is still difficult. Trans-abdominal ultrasound may be utilized with tractable females (those used to human touch).

There is very little data from either captive or field studies about the reproductive physiology of male okapis. They appear to reach sexual maturity a little later than do females. There does not appear to be any evidence that sperm production or fertility in captive males is seasonal. However, some individuals have been reported to cease sperm production for several months.

Walking through a break in the Ituri Forest.

Male okapi behind a tree trunk.

In the wild, males have home ranges that often overlap with those of several females. Okapis from adjacent home ranges often travel along the same paths. Captive okapis frequently sample the urine and feces of others via olfactory and gustatory means. It is likely that the males can ascertain the reproductive status of the females via olfactory evaluation of urine, feces, and possibly pedal gland deposits along these shared pathways. Males will exhibit an exaggerated *flehmen* response (a distinctive behavioral response involving raising of head, flaring of nostrils, and rolling back of the lips) to the urine of receptive females. Recently there has been speculation that vocalizations within the infrasound range (inaudible to humans) may well aid in uniting potential mates.

Okapis have a variety of audible (to humans) and inaudible calls. When okapis first meet, they will often emit a cough call, or "chuff." The most frequent vocalization given by adults and young, this contact

Male testing a female's urine.

Male displaying a flehmen response, with nostrils flared and lips rolled back.

call is often reciprocal. A male that is attempting to approach a female will circle her in smaller and smaller circles, holding his head high and often vocalizing in a distinctive manner, termed a groan or "moan." This vocalization, which has been noted in captivity with a few males and confirmed by researchers at the Epulu compound, is heard only during courtship and breeding.

Female and male okapis meeting.

Once the pair is in proximity, both will begin to olfactorily and tactilely explore one another while circling. The female may periodically lie down in a sternal or lateral position, raising or lowering her head during the encounter. The male will attempt to encourage her to rise by kicking at her with a foreleg or butting her sides (flanks) and rump with his horns. Occasionally when the female again stands, she will gallop away a short distance with the male following. Commonly, a receptive pair will assume a reverse parallel position, mutually sniffing genital regions as they circle one another. The female may lick the penile sheath of the male, who often dribbles urine which the female will sample. When the female urinates, the male reciprocates. Flehmen responses are seen in both sexes.

Early courtship behavior.

Male "chest-rests" against female as he laufschlags and tests her readiness to breed.

As familiarity and excitement increase, other behaviors are seen. While standing behind the female, the male exhibits various erect and stretched postures with his head and neck, while the female generally displays a head-low posture. More contact ensues, with the male chest-resting against the female's hindquarters while he directs leg kicks, or *laufschlags*, toward her rear. Periodically he will attempt to mount her and will vocalize more frequently. A nonreceptive female may step forward away from the male or kick backward. If the female is receptive, she will stand solidly with tail averted during mounting attempts. Copulation will occur during one of these attempts and is terminated by the female walking away.

The mating period in captivity is artificially determined; however, in the wild it appears to be relatively brief, encompassing a few days at most. Both male and female will then continue their solitary ways until the next breeding encounter or the female gives birth to a calf.

Gestation averages 14.5 months (440 days), and some females appear to cycle even after impregnation. This phenomenon has resulted in widely varying estimates of gestation. Females have also been successfully reim-

Male mounts standing female.

pregnated as early as one month after giving birth (during a post-partum estrus).

In captivity, calving may occur throughout the year, although many institutions make an attempt to breed their okapi on a schedule that results in spring or summer births. Due to their habitat, unique coloration, and behavioral adaptations, the okapi is one of the most difficult animals to observe in the wild. Natural history information is garnered from tracks and radio telemetry, and our knowledge about reproduction in the wild is limited. John and Terese Hart lived at Epulu for many years while studying the okapi. They noted that calves may be born anytime of year but are most common during the two dry seasons (December through February and June through August).

In the wild, the female okapi probably withdraws from other okapis (adults and possibly an older offspring) prior to giving birth. This behavior has been observed among females in the compounds at Epulu. In captivity, pregnant females are often separated from other okapis by the tenth month of gestation, although some institutions may isolate the

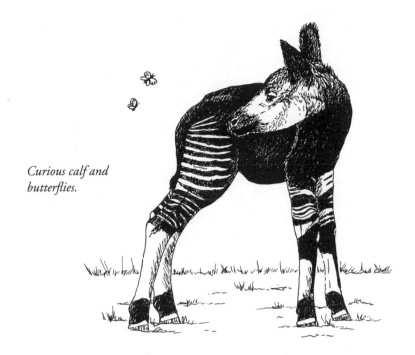

Curious calf and butterflies.

expectant mother only at night. Preparations also may include setting aside two adjoining stalls for the expectant mother. In the wild, the female will not stay constantly with her calf but will feed and rest out of the calf's sight. An extra stall allows the pair to simulate this separation in captivity, as they are not forced into constant contact.

When given both indoor and outdoor access, okapis may deliver outdoors and away from the peripheral paths that they normally travel in their enclosures. Distension of the belly, an enlarged vulva, a slight discharge, holding the tail up, and restlessness characterize the beginning of the birth process (parturition). The female may pace or lie and rise repeatedly throughout the birth. Usually births are single and the calf is presented head and forelegs first (as if diving into a new world) as is observed in most ungulates. Any other orientation may be problematic. The mother is usually standing and may circle as the calf is expelled still enclosed within the amniotic sac and with the umbilical cord intact. From the time that contractions are seen until the birth of the calf, two to four hours may elapse, although the time varies widely.

Most mothers lick the perineal area and consume the (amniotic) fluids and fetal membranes. They will also consume the placenta, which is usually expelled within two hours after birth. It is thought that some nutritional or hormonal benefits result from this behavior. It may also afford a measure of protection against predators who might otherwise be drawn to the spot where the calf was born or later hidden.

Nearby captive okapis and other ungulates appear to be excited by the birth odors or sounds even when they are unable to see the actual birth. Other okapis often "chuff" or cough call in the direction of the mother and calf. The mother may or may not respond vocally. Newborns are capable of cough calls and will also "bleat" when stressed.

The average newborn okapi calf weighs 49.5 pounds (22.5 kg), and weights taken within twenty-four hours of birth range from 32 to 69.5 pounds (14.57–31.59 kg). At birth, the diminutive and vulnerable calf will be lying on its side. It appears wet and dark in color, and its ears are plastered to its head. The neonate will struggle to raise its head and to place its legs beneath it (the position described as sternal). It quickly accomplishes this with its front legs, but the splaying hind legs are more difficult to control. Many tries later, the calf manages to get its hind feet squarely under its body so that it is in a position to attempt to stand.

Sternal calf.

Interspersed with licking herself and consuming membranes, the mother will usually be solicitous toward her calf. She will nuzzle and lick the calf while it attempts to free itself from any amniotic sac remnants. Usually after the consumption of the afterbirth, the mother gives her full attention to cleansing the calf. During this critical period, it is believed that the calf and mother become familiar with each other's scent through olfactory and gustatory cues.

Mother cleaning newborn.

While being cleansed, the calf will attempt to become sternal and to rise to its feet. Okapi newborns are precocial (exhibiting an advanced degree of independent activity at birth). The "average" okapi calf assumes the sternal position within eight minutes after birth. Its first attempts to stand usually occur within twelve minutes after birth, and it may stand successfully for the first time within twenty-nine minutes. Throughout all this activity the mother continues to groom and nuzzle the calf, perhaps encouraging its attempts to stand. Calves that are not with solicitous mothers often take longer to reach these developmental landmarks. Splaying or slipping on slick floors has been an ongoing problem for calves born in captivity. Crushed limestone or similar material may be used on the floor of maternal stalls in order to afford better traction for small wet hooves. The ability to stand soon after birth is essential to survival in the wild; it may also be critical in captivity. Mothers have been reported to be highly aggressive toward calves that are splayed and struggling.

When dry, the calf is a rich blackish brown color with shaggy white striped hindquarters and legs, lacking the sleek appearance of the mother. The calf's finely furred coat appears darker than an adult's and there is a starburst pattern surrounding its eyes. A short mane or mantle starts between the ears and runs down its head, back and to the rump. The young okapi has thick, long legs but a small head and short neck.

Newborn Katala with floppy ears.

*Mother grooming back
of nursing calf.*

First attempts to walk usually result in falls. It takes several days to
perfect a steady walk. During this time, the walk is wobbly and unstable.
First steps are in an alternating walk pattern, not the lateral or parallel gait
found in giraffes and adult okapis. The average calf will first attempt to
nurse within thirty-eight minutes and is successful by seventy-seven minutes following birth, although this varies greatly. Some calves have trouble
finding their mother's udder and will nose and lick all around her body
for a place to nurse. Inexperienced mothers may not readily tolerate such
contact. Once nursing has begun, the mother usually grooms the calf
around its rump and perineal area (between the anus and external genita-
lia). Initially, nursing sessions may be as frequent as five times each hour.

The mother has four teats, and the calf will often switch among them during long nursing bouts. In addition, the calf bunts, or butts, its mother's udder, presumably to encourage faster milk "let down." The intensity and frequency of bunting increases as the calf ages. The usual sucking position of the young is termed the reverse parallel position and is exhibited by most bovids and giraffes. In this classic position the calf's rear is oriented toward the mother's head. However, the calf may nurse in numerous other positions—including from between mom's rear legs.

During nursing bouts, the newborn calf receives colostrum from its mother. This secretion precedes milk, which is produced within a few days of delivery. Unlike milk, the main components of colostrum are serum and white blood corpuscles. This is how the calf receives passive immunity to certain diseases from its mother. Survival rates of captive-born calves have been relatively low. Speculation regarding the high mortality rate has included inbreeding and susceptibility to bacterial infections during the first year of life. Since 1978, the number of highly inbred newborns has declined, thanks to the inception of a special breeding plan (SSP, see chapter 5), but the mortality rate of okapis in the first year of life remains high. In the past ten years, there has been a 21 percent probability that a newborn in the North American population will not survive its first year of life; this increases to 40 percent for calves born in Europe. Calves born to primiparous females (first-time mothers) appear to be at greatest risk. The reason is unclear but seems to include inexperience and lower birth weights. Male calves born in captivity, regardless of birth order, also appear to be at higher risk. While first-year mortality is higher for males than females, the first ten days of life appear to be especially critical for all calves.

Most mothers are extremely protective of their newborns and react aggressively toward any approach to them. The mothers often respond similarly toward any loud noise. Because of this aggression and the importance of establishing a solid bond between mother and calf, the mother and her newborn in captivity are usually not disturbed and the area kept relatively quiet.

Some mothers respond inappropriately to their newborns, either ignoring the calf or directing aggressive behaviors such as kicks and stomps toward it. If the calf's life appears to be overly threatened and the mother's behavior continues to be inappropriate, the calf may be removed from

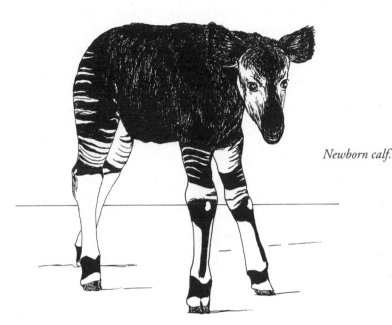

Newborn calf.

its mother in an attempt to hand raise it. Maternal aggression resulted in the death of the first okapi born in Europe, at Antwerp in 1954, and again occurred in 1956. A female at the Brookfield Zoo has attacked several of her offspring. It is speculated that these mothers had an inherent tendency toward aggression or that this behavior resulted from the stressful and foreign state of captivity. However, recent events suggest that these animals could be reacting to the reception of confusing and possibly threatening sounds. An experienced mother at Brookfield, possibly startled by the cries of a human infant, attacked her seventh calf, which was then six days old. An incident in Copenhagen resulted in a mother's death, reportedly due to stress following a loud musical rehearsal (possibly with infrasonic components; see later in this chapter). In Dallas, females with calves showed signs of stress when exposed to live music nearby. Luckily, none of these incidents were severe enough to threaten the lives of the calves.

Usually, no human contact is made with the calf until twenty-four to forty-eight hours after birth, when a neonatal (newborn) exam may be performed. However, a calf that suffers maternal rejection or exhibits signs of a severe health problem may need to be hand-reared. Historically, hand-rearing has not been very successful, probably due in part to supply problems and a lack of understanding of the composition of okapi milk. The milk is believed to have approximately one-third greater concentration of protein than cow's milk and a lower fat content. In recent years, Brookfield, Dallas, and Marwell in Great Britain have successfully hand-reared calves on a mixture of canned evaporated milk, powdered cow's milk replacer, and water. One wonders how similar this formula is to the mixture of condensed milk and cow's milk used by Mrs. Landeghem with Buta, the first successfully hand-reared calf.

The okapi calf appears to be rather unique in certain aspects of its physiological and behavioral ontogeny (development). Among its unusual characteristics are rapid initial growth rate, delay in defecation, inefficient stabilization of body temperature, and distinctive nesting stages. The significance of findings concerning these developmental aspects is still being discussed.

The average okapi calf doubles its birth weight in twenty-eight days and triples its weight within forty-nine days. This rate of growth exceeds

Mother and calf grooming each other.

that of animals of similar size and type. Calves fail to regularly produce feces for a prolonged period of time, usually well over one month. The mechanism for this delay is not understood. Before okapi calves had been extensively studied in captivity, it was thought that the mother licked out and consumed the feces. However, meconium (waste mass which accumulates in the fetal bowel and is discharged after birth), which has a distinctive appearance, has been collected from healthy okapi ranging between twenty-eight and seventy-four (average 42.5) days old. Not knowing about this unique aspect of okapi physiology, many veterinarians attempted to give the calf some relief from an apparent case of constipation. Unfortunately, the removal of this material may have contributed to early infections.

Some researchers attribute the okapi calf's rapid growth and delayed defecation to the extremely efficient use of its mother's milk. Hand-reared calves generally start defecating early and regularly and may not attain the same growth rate as mother-reared animals. Early defecation in a mother-reared calf (especially within the first ten days of life), is most often associated with a health problem in the developing neonate. It is interesting to note that okapi calves begin to freely defecate at about the same time that the intensive nesting phase ends (between six and nine weeks of age) and they begin to move around. Such an unusual developmental phenomenon undoubtedly has adaptive value; perhaps it allows for a rapid postpartum growth period, or provides additional concealment against detection by predators, or both.

Okapi calves, like most mammalian neonates, do not rigorously thermoregulate (stabilize their body temperatures). Outside a narrow range, their body temperature tends to drift toward the ambient (surrounding) temperature. We found that body temperatures for okapi calves average 38.07°C (100.5°F) over the first ninety days of life. Okapi calves appear to take up to two months (fifty-one to sixty days) to narrowly thermoregulate. This time period coincides approximately with the end of the intensive nesting phase, when most calves increase their activity levels.

The okapi is an intermediate hider/follower that exhibits three or four distinctive nesting stages. For the first seventy-two hours, the calf is very active, often initiating contact with the mother and exploring its surroundings. This stage may be adaptive in that it gives the mother and calf a chance to remove themselves from a birth site that might attract predators. The calf will rest in several locations during the first seventy-two hours but eventually selects a specific site to which it will constantly return. This signals the beginning of the intensive nesting stage, which lasts until the calf is approximately six to nine weeks old. During this period, the calf spends most of its time standing or lying on the nest. Contact with the mother consists mostly of nursing episodes.

Growth is rapid, thermoregulation is perfected, the rumen is activated, and the meconium is passed as the calf emerges from this stage. From week nine through twenty-four, the calf gradually begins to spend more and more time off the nest and in social contact with its mother. This period represents a gradual withdrawal from the nest. There is some

Okapi calf sleeping on its nest in the Ituri.

speculation that okapi milk composition changes with each nesting stage of development.

Hungry okapi calves will rise from lying on the nest in response to the sight or vocalizations of the mother. These vocalizations may be humanly audible or infrasonic. The mother may also nose and lick the calf while it is on the nest in order to initiate a nursing bout. The mother most frequently initiates nursing bouts during the intensive nesting phase. Later the calf may begin to initiate the majority of nursing interactions.

Calf initiating play or nursing.

Usually, the mother will groom her calf while it nurses. Unfortunately, some mothers will overgroom the perineal skin of their offspring until it becomes sore or inflamed. This results in extreme discomfort for the calf and may also cause constipation. In very severe cases, licking with the mother's raspy tongue results in swelling that closes off the rectum and may result in death. In 1988 the San Diego Wild Animal Park constructed a coat that protected a calf's sensitive areas from an overzealous mother's tongue. This intervention allowed animal care personnel to leave the infant with its mother until it was old enough to be weaned. Time of weaning varies but is usually artificially imposed between six and eight months in captivity—especially when overgrooming problems develop. Overgrooming occurs most frequently during extended periods of confinement or when space restrictions do not allow two stalls and the mother and calf cannot separate visually. Unfortunately, mothers that develop a tendency to overgroom one calf are likely to repeat the behavior with subsequent calves. Increasing the amount of space available to okapi mothers and their calves has substantially decreased the incidence of this problem and the deaths attributed to it.

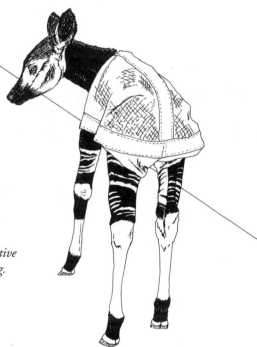

San Diego Wild Animal Park's calf wearing protective coat against overgrooming.

Habituation to contact, especially leg manipulation, has been demonstrated as important with captive okapis. Frequently irregular growth and other hoof problems have been noted. It is desirable to be able to work with the animals—such as applying a rasp to overgrown areas of a hoof—without having to physically or chemically (drug) restrain them. By gradually habituating a newborn calf to human contact, one gains a more steady, tractable animal and one that will tolerate necessary minor procedures in the absence of restraint. Okapis seem to be very sensitive, and their reaction to medication, which is not always predictable, can result in the loss of an animal. Habituation of calves to contact has also allowed for the collection of other important physiological data of a type that previously could be collected only from stressed or ill animals. The habituation process can occur during periods when the mother naturally separates herself from her calf. The calf may be found on the nest while the female is usually occupied in another stall or outside. This minimizes stress and impact on nursing patterns. Over the course of several days, the keeper attempts to approach the calf and touch it. Each day more time is spent with the calf until it regularly allows the approach. The keeper begins to touch the animal until it will tolerate manipulation of its legs and the application of hoof implements. It is even possible to collect rectal temperatures this way. Calves that have been habituated to contact quickly accept touching on the perineum and the brief insertion of a thermometer. Some animals will continue to tolerate this procedure into adulthood, others for a few months only. Individual temperament of the okapi calf plays an important role, as does the measure of trust between the keeper and the animal.

Keeper rasping okapi calf's rear hoof.

Keeper preparing to take a calf's rectal temperature.

Knowledge about the okapi calf's nesting behavior has also been utilized to collect daily weights. Captive calves tend to nest under or near fixed stall features such as feeding trays and hay racks. At the Dallas Zoo, triangular platforms are placed in the corner of the stall, and most calves will choose one to nest under as their semipermanent nest site. As the calf grows, the platform is raised to accommodate the animal and to discourage relocation of the nest. Also, as the calf grows, weight is obtained from a platform scale that has been placed under the nest hay. The calf can be weighed prior to and after nursing without disturbing its usual pattern of activity and contact with its mother. Information regarding amount of milk consumed (as much as four pounds [1.78 kg] during a single nursing episode) and growth rates has been obtained in this manner. As the calf ages, it can be trained to walk on a larger platform scale located in a passage leading to the exhibit area. Weights can be collected on somewhat tractable individuals throughout their lives. This is particularly important through pregnancy and the period of lactation.

By using inherent okapi behavior to the best advantage, more has

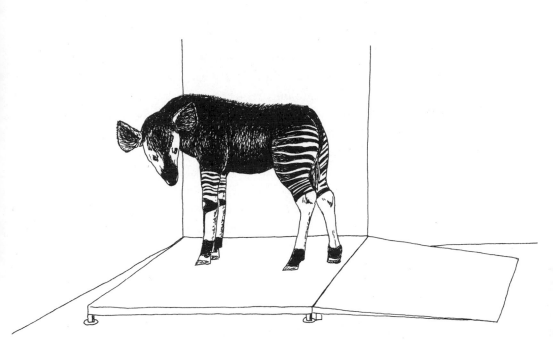

Calf standing on platform scale in nesting area.

been learned about this species than would have been possible in their dense native habitat. In fact, our study of captive newborns at the Dallas Zoo led to the discovery that these animals use infrasound to communicate in a manner previously undocumented. This could ultimately be useful in garnering knowledge about population levels and behavior of okapi in the wild. An understanding of this secret language of the okapi may also assist in helping to alleviate overly stressful situations in captivity, such as those which may have contributed to the death of some individuals.

We first began to speculate that infrasound may be used by okapi calves and their mothers in 1990. It was frequently noted that animals synchronized behavior, but the observers could discern no obvious behavioral cues. For example, three related female okapis, including a newborn only several hours old, were housed in two adjoining areas and were observed to move simultaneously toward a common door. This coordinated movement was not preceded by any overt behavior or humanly audible vocalization. Upon reaching the solid, closed door, the two older females emitted chuffs toward one another while the calf stood nearby.

Further, an ongoing study of okapi mothers and infants had also revealed that behaviors such as "chuff" vocalizations, nuzzling, and becoming visible were used to initiate nursing only 1 to 2 percent of the time. The initiator of all other nursing bouts could not be identified. Previously, researchers at Brookfield had indicated that a high percentage of "chuff" calls initiated nursing. In 1992, recordings of ten okapis at the San Diego Wild Animal Park and the White Oak Conservation Center (in Yulee, Florida) were made by Dr. Joseph Daniel, Jr., Elizabeth von Muggenthaler, and John K. Pritchard, and these tapes first revealed that this species produces low frequency sounds in the 9 to 70 hertz (cycles per second) range.

Calf responding to mom's call.

Forest elephants.

With few exceptions, the most sensitive human ear cannot perceive frequencies below 20 hertz. Frequencies in this range are called infrasound. Unbeknownst to us, the physical world throbs with infrasonic noises produced by thunder, air turbulence, jet engines, volcanoes, earthquakes, ocean waves, and buildings. In the biological world, however, the ability to produce or perceive infrasound has been considered a rarity. Early bioacoustic research with marine mammals showed that many of the recorded songs of blue whales ranged partially into infrasonic frequencies. Elephants were the first terrestrial mammals reported to produce low-frequency vocalizations. Infrasound has now been documented in okapis and the four species of rhinoceros (black, white, Sumatran, and Indian). It is also reported in various birds, reptiles, and insects.

There are a number of advantages to communicating in infrasound. Its longer wavelengths dissipate less over distance and resist being scattered by trees and hills. The source of a low-frequency sound is more difficult to locate than that of a higher-frequency sound and could reduce predation risk. The possibility exists that infrasound provides a major vehicle by which animals convey information both within and across species. For example, they may identify themselves to conspecifics, initiate interactions, space themselves, and safely announce behavioral events, such as birth or readiness to mate. Infrasound could be especially useful to an animal such as the okapi that is primarily solitary, lives in a dense habitat, uses widely spaced territories, and experiences a degree of predation pressure.

At both the Dallas Zoo and the White Oak Conservation Center, we have documented that okapis emit copious amounts of low-frequency sounds. Mother-calf pairs (or dyads) often use infrasonic calls to initiate nursing. These signals have frequencies of 30 hertz and below, with the strongest amplitudes primarily at 12 to 15 hertz. These signals are most frequently emitted when there is no visual contact between the mother and calf and may result in one disclosing its location or one approaching the other for nursing.

Mother grooms back of nursing calf.

Several distinct types of purely infrasonic calls have been recorded. One call, which was recorded when one of the mothers became startled by an unidentified stimulus, may represent an alarm vocalization. Also, two adult males housed at the Dallas Zoo emitted periodic, repetitive, and distinctive infrasonic calls during evenings while pacing (strongest amplitudes primarily at 15 to 17 hertz). Calls such as these might also be useful in helping to space adult male okapis in the wild, since they traverse the boundaries of their home ranges more frequently than do females and subadult males. The cough call, or "chuff," may be emitted with or without an infrasonic leader component. This probably explains the phenomenon we first observed and speculated about in 1990. It is hoped that continued analysis will further elucidate the private language of the okapi. In fact, playback of infrasonic calls along home range boundaries may well hold promise for obtaining a more accurate census of okapis in the wild.

This unique species remains a genetic enigma. Most mammals have a distinct number of chromosomes and a constant diploid (2n) number. For example, humans have 23 pairs of chromosomes and a constant diploid number, 2n = 46. Any variance from this number is abnormal and often results in death or a very severe physical or mental defect. In the okapi, there appears to be a variance in the 2n number. Okapis were originally thought to have 2n = 46; however, later analysis revealed some animals with 2n = 45. Animals with either number appear normal.

Aneuploid organisms have a chromosome number that is not an exact multiple of the basic set. One of the common forms is trisomy, where an extra chromosome is present, such as in Down's syndrome (Trisomy 21). Monosomy, such as is exhibited by okapis with 2n = 45, is a form of aneuploidy in which one copy of the chromosome is missing. It is believed that a translocation across the ends of the short arms of nonhomologous chromosomes (such as the sex chromosomes x and y) has occurred in the 2n = 45 animals. This type of monosomy is often called Robertsonian fusion. Okapis carrying either 45 or 46 chromosomes can produce healthy viable offspring. Researchers have speculated that the variance in diploid number might account for some spontaneous reabsorptions or abortions. In fact, there appears to be a difference in the urinary profiles (pregnanediol-3-glucuronide) of okapis with different karyotypes.

Playful calf.

An attempt has been made to karyotype each captive okapi in order to discern more about the variation in chromosomal numbers. This requires a sample of blood or skin (usually from the back of an ear). In 1991 this procedure had been completed with the majority of the animals held in the United States. Any banked blood or tissue samples from deceased animals have also been tested. The 1996 International Studbook indicates that forty okapis had a 2n = 46 and forty-six had a 2n = 45. Two animals with 2n = 44 also have been found. Current husbandry practices require that all newborn okapis be karyotyped in hopes that we might someday better understand this mystery.

4. Field Studies

Okapis are limited (endemic) to the rain forests of northeastern Congo-Zaire and commonly range at altitudes between 1,650 and 3,300 feet (500–1,000 meters). Their habitat does not include the high montane forest in the east, the western swamp forests, the northern savanna, or the southern open woodlands. The open savanna is more suited to their closest relative, the giraffe. Okapi have always been most common in the Wamba and Epulu areas of the Ituri Forest, and most of the animals found in zoos are descendants of animals captured near Epulu.

In 1928 Camp Putnam, or Epulu, was founded in the Ituri Forest by Patrick Putnam. Here he also built a small hotel and thatched cottages for the interesting guests that he hoped would visit, and a village grew up around him. Putnam operated a clinic for the local people and built a school for the children. He also kept some of the local fauna, including

Male okapi walking by fallen trees in open area of the forest.

okapis, in a fenced area. An eccentric, undisciplined genius, Pat Putnam became an expert on the pygmy life-style and the Ituri Forest.

Jean de Medina, a retired Belgian officer, became the director of the Fish and Game Administration's capture station at Epulu in 1948. He fenced in about ten acres (0.4 hectacres) of forest along the Epulu River to hold his private collection of animals—including breeding pairs of okapis. Once a professional hunter for the colonial railroad, de Medina captured Congo peacock, gorilla, and okapi on behalf of the Belgian colonial administration for export to European and American zoos. This continued until the early 1960s, when the country became independent. The station would not be used again until 1965, when he returned at the request of the Zaire National Parks Institute. De Medina's replacement, Jean Bosco, collected okapis until 1973, and after that time only one okapi was exported until 1984. Since 1987, the Epulu Conservation and Research Center has been run by a Swiss couple, Rosemarie and Karl Ruf. The majority of the research on the okapi in this area has been undertaken during their tenure.

Drs. John and Terese Hart, a zoologist and a botanist from Michigan State University, first visited Epulu in 1973. They returned in 1980, acquired the Putnam homestead, and built a house and research station along the Epulu River approximately one mile away from Epulu. The Harts began their work on okapi in 1986 with funding from the Wildlife Conservation International Division of the New York Zoological Society. Their research focused on the status, biology, and conservation of the okapi in the Ituri Forest and concentrated on a 17.4-square-mile (45 km²) study area northwest of Epulu. Between 1986 and 1993, the Harts placed radio collars on twenty-five free-ranging animals. Twenty-two okapis were monitored systematically for periods ranging from three months to over four years. A map-grid system was used to track the okapis, and most animals were approachable. In fact, the Harts and their assistants found that lactating females were so busy eating that they paid little attention to nearby researchers. Five radio collars were replaced during the study; they generally lasted less than three years.

Many native scholars have assisted the Harts in gathering, describing, and documenting the vegetation of the Ituri. Perhaps the Harts' most significant finding is that much of the wild okapi's behavior may be limited by habitat and food. They found that the leaves of more than two hundred species of dicotyledonous plant (a plant having two seed leaves) make up the diet of wild okapis, and only thirty species constitute the staples. Generally, monocots (a plant having one seed leaf, such as grasses, corn, and lilies) are not eaten, nor are the common understory or dominant canopy seedlings. The diet of wild okapis consists entirely of foliage; this diet makes the okapi unique among the inhabitants of the Ituri Forest. Most of the ungulates that share the forest are fruit eaters (frugivores). The okapi is a highly selective browser that prefers fast-growing, sun-loving species found in the forest openings created by fallen trees (5 percent of forest areas studied were treefalls, but these were the majority of okapi feeding areas). For this reason, although okapis occur in higher densities in primary forest cover, the researchers found that these animals frequently forage in secondary growth and along stream beds. The peak activity and feeding times are mid-morning and late afternoon. Some movement was seen on moonlit nights.

*Female okapi reaching for
leaves in a tree.*

*Male feeding on
low bush.*

The Harts found that wild lactating females increase their forage intake, spend more time browsing, and use a greater range of browse species during the six months when their calves are nursing. Epulu Compound researchers concurrently noted that captive, lactating females increase forage intake by 60 to 80 percent over nonlactating females. Calves stay on secluded nests within their mother's home range while she feeds nearby. It has been reported that females will allow nursing from calves other than their own and may actually adopt calves. Okapis generally give birth to one calf while secluded from conspecifics. Unlike herd animals, there would be no need to evolve an immediate and irrevocable bonding response. For this reason, both at Epulu Compound and in captivity, it is advisable that the mother and calf be confined together, away from others, until the more elongated bonding process has been completed. In the wild, offspring may remain with, or near, their mother until they are weaned at approximately six months or until the mother gives birth again. One radio-collared calf was independent at approximately nine months of age. What prompts a calf to leave its mother's home range has not been determined. Two radio-collared juveniles (less than one year old) both restricted their movements to the mother's home range during the course of the Harts' study. Subadults (less than three years old) of both sexes apparently travel over large distances in what may constitute dispersal from the natal home ranges. Five radio-collared subadults all disappeared from the study area. One was found dead; three others were located by aerial search as much as 15.5 miles (25 km) from where they were originally caught.

Mom and calf.

Okapis are apparently not territorial in the sense that they do not directly defend an area against the intrusion of conspecifics. They have home ranges that often overlap and that provide the necessities of water, food, and shelter. Adult males are wide ranging, and their home ranges, which may be 3 to 4.6 square miles (8–12 km²) in size, are less well defined than those of females. In a day, males cover greater distances, up to 5 miles (8 km), as compared to under 1.2 miles (2 km) for females. The Harts found that, as compared to males, both females and subadults (of both sexes) had smaller home ranges. Breeding females had the best-defined ranges, which were stable year after year and covered from 1.2 to 2 square miles (3 km²–5.5 km²).

John and Terese Hart believe that there is evidence that a dominance relationship of some sort may exist among familiar male okapis. Although the observed adult males were wide ranging, and their home ranges appeared to be nonexclusive, few conflicts between radio-collared males occurred. However, two were seen chasing each other, and wounds caused by horns were seen on the bodies of others. Several males were found near a mother and her calf, presumably attracted by the female's post-partum estrus. Since okapis are generally solitary, male and female associations of a few days duration are common only during the female's estrus.

Subadult (subdominant) or adult males ranged widely and were more likely to emigrate from the study area. Emigration generally makes an animal more vulnerable to predation. Leopard attacks are a significant cause of mortality for wild okapis. Approximately 25 percent of the study area subadults (of both sexes) and adult males were depredated. Breeding females who remained within their home ranges appeared to be much

Male, female, and calf sharing the same range.

Leopard crouching in tree.

less vulnerable. Captured okapis frequently have scars from unsuccessful leopard attacks. Epulu reported attacks of a leopard on two occasions in 1957, each resulting in the death of a young okapi. The Harts lost three of their collared study animals in 1986. Of the thirty-one okapis captured in the Ituri as part of the Epulu captive breeding work, one female was chased into a pit and killed by a leopard.

The natives of the Epulu area have traditionally utilized three methods when capturing animals: pit traps, net snare, and vertical nets. Vertical nets are spread out, the animals are driven into them, and the prey become entangled and are usually killed. This method is used most often to capture forest duikers for food. Net snares are laid flat on the ground in animal pathways. A trench covered with foliage is hidden below the snare. When the prey steps on the snare, the net closes. Once the animal sinks into the trench, it is killed by the natives. The pit trap requires much more work and is generally used for larger prey—such as the okapi.

Okapis follow regular pathways through the forest within their home ranges. The Mbuti place modified traditional, camouflaged, pitfall traps along these trails. This has long been the major means of capture for okapis. Without the assistance of the natives, it is unlikely that the Harts'

*Okapi calf in
a boma.*

research could have been carried out or that there would be any okapis
in captivity.

During modern capture campaigns, approximately 150 pit traps are
dug in groups of 10 along pathways frequented by okapis. Pit traps for
okapi measure approximately two to three feet wide, six feet long, and
six feet deep (.9 x 1.8 x 1.8 m, respectively). A thick layer of sand covers
the bottom to cushion the okapi's fall. The opening is camouflaged with
sticks and leaves, which also help to prevent injury during the fall, and
the area is swept so no human traces remain. The pit is checked several
times a day to prevent leopards or driver ants from finding the helpless
okapi first. When an animal is found in the pit, the opening is covered
up with twigs and leaves. Darkness has a calming effect on the animal so
that it is less likely to exhaust itself in its attempts to escape. If the okapi
is to be radio-collared, the collar is placed from behind a screen of leaves;
then dirt is shoveled into the pit to create a ramp up which the animal
can escape. Otherwise, if the animal is to be held, a *boma,* or sturdy stick
corral, is constructed. It takes five to six hours to build a boma that is
approximately fifty feet (15 m) in diameter and has an open side facing

the pit trap. A dirt ramp is created within the pit and a short, narrow transfer alley is built between the pit and the *boma*. Browse and a bucket of water on the inside of the boma help to encourage the okapi to enter. Mbuti guards are stationed nearby to protect the okapi from leopard attack. The okapi in the pit usually is not aggressive but, rather, tired and calm. Once the animal is in the corral, one crew starts to cut a "road" through the forest while another builds a loading ramp. A truck that is outfitted with a transport cage padded with plant material and jute is backed up to the ramp. The okapi tends to seek the dark and moves up into the crate as leaves are removed from the boma. The animal is then transported by truck for three to five hours from the capture point to the station; there the entire process is reversed, with the okapi being lured from truck to corral. Once settled at Epulu, the okapi is assigned to a specific keeper. Slowly, visual barriers are reduced until the okapi is

Okapi investigates shipping crate.

comfortable in a chain link enclosure. In about two months, the okapi has acclimated to captivity and is often quite gentle.

Okapis housed in zoological institutions around the world represent both a hedge against extinction and important ambassadors for the wild population and their forest home. Because the captive population descends from a small number of animals all captured within a limited area, it requires an occasional influx of new genetic material to broaden its genetic base and to prevent inbreeding and its associated problems. In 1996 geneticists projected that six okapis would be needed over the next ten years as founders (unrelated genetic stock) for the captive group.

Wild-caught okapis are held temporarily at Epulu as breeding stock and are then returned to their forest home. Females may be housed together; however, males are confined alone, since fights between rivals have occurred. The breeding pair is separated once it is clear that the female has conceived. The Epulu-reared captive offspring adapt more readily to crate confinement, human manipulation, and other shipping requirements for exportation. Shipment of only tamer, Epulu-reared okapis lessens the risk to the animal and thus helps to ensure that a genetically viable captive reserve can be propagated while mitigating the deleterious effects on the wild population. Should human encroachment and exploitation decimate the only rain forest where the okapi is found, the captive population may serve as a reservoir for preservation of this species.

Male okapi looking backward.

5. Conservation

With the largest share of intact tropical rain forest of any country in Africa, the Democratic Republic of Congo is important for the conservation of biodiversity. Home to more species of vertebrates than anywhere else on the continent, Congo-Zaire ranks first in mammals (409 species), birds (1,086), and amphibians (216), and second in reptile species (280). It also has the most swallowtail butterflies in Africa (48 species) and ranks second for flowering plants (about 10,800). Within the Zaire River Basin alone, there are over 270 species of mammals and 150 species of birds, as well as 700 species of ants and thousands of other insects. The vegetation is also distinctive, with many endemic species. No one knows how many species have yet to be discovered, described, and saved.

Some butterflies of Congo-Zaire. In descending order: Papilio zalmoxis, Papilio phorcas, Druryeia antimachus, Papilio phorcas (wings folded).

Bonobos, the okapi's neighbors.

Among the unique fauna of Congo-Zaire is the bonobo, or pygmy chimpanzee, which lives across the Zaire River south of the Ituri Forest. It was first recognized as a separate species of chimpanzee in 1933. This chimp is slender and dark-faced, and the hair on top of its head projects sideways in tufts. Bonobo adults maintain the white "tail-tuft" that, among common chimpanzees, is usually found only in juveniles. Only about 15,000 bonobos are left in the wild, and approximately 100 in captivity. Studies are underway, but little is yet known about this unique species.

Another Ituri native, the Congo peacock has been protected by the government since 1938. First exhibited at the New York Zoo in 1947, when seven birds were exported, today they are found in many other zoos in the United States. Tree hyrax, African gray parrot, green turaco, black-and-white colobus monkey, dwarf galago, forest elephant, bongo, yellow-backed duiker, water chevrotain, African golden cat, pangolin, and leopard are only a small representative group of the bird and mammal fauna that depend upon this land area for their survival.

The okapi, although sparsely distributed, is not rare within its range. It is estimated that 10,000 to 20,000 okapis remain in an area centered on the Ituri Forest in northeastern Congo-Zaire. The Ituri is one of the largest remnants of Congo Basin rain forest and represents a regional center of biodiversity.

Since the okapi's discovery in 1901, the Western world has shown great interest in this endemic species. Sir Harry Johnston himself, in his letter and article for *The Times* (March 31, 1901), urged the Belgian monarchy to adopt measures against the extermination of okapis. In his book *The Uganda Protectorate*, at the end of the section on okapi, Johnston wrote:

> It is because of human actions that the Mammoth, the European Bison, the Quagga, the Dodo and Giant Auk died out. The defenseless Okapi was only able to stay alive because it withdrew to the densest parts of the Congo forest, where Lions could not penetrate and the Leopard lives in the trees and hunts Monkeys. The only human enemies used to be just the pygmies, and a few Bantu living at the edge of the forest. The question now is for how long will the Okapi be able to keep living, since the natives now have guns, and the trophy collectors are hunting for this special animal. It is to be hoped that the British and Belgian governments will cooperate to protect the Okapi from extinction.

Rain forest residents.

In ensuing years, the Belgian government would pass a variety of resolutions and regulations that required licenses for hunting and capturing animals in Congo-Zaire, then known as the Belgian Free Congo. However, the okapi was not specifically listed for protection until 1933. On November 8 of that year, the okapi was put on the list of fully protected animals compiled by the first International Convention for the Protection of Fauna and Flora, held in London. This action was ratified by Belgium on July 22, 1935. Henceforth, the okapi could be captured or killed only by the permission of the highest authorities. The former Belgian Colonial Administration gave okapis exclusively to zoos of scientific importance. In modern times, the Zairian government maintained a "monopoly" on okapis. Today, the okapi is protected as a national treasure in the Democratic Republic of Congo.

Frequently depicted on postal stamps and other Zairian, Belgian, and European artwork, the okapi unfortunately remains unknown to much of the Western world. Most people have never heard of an okapi, and if they do know what it is, they have never seen it. Lang's statement that those who "have seen a living okapi . . . have been so favored" still rings true.

In 1981 the American Zoo and Aquarium Association established a cooperative population management program called the Species Survival Plan (SSP) for the breeding of threatened and endangered animals in

Treasure of Congo-Zaire.

captivity. This planned management helps to maintain a genetically diverse, healthy, stable, and self-sustaining population. As of 1994 there were 110 species covered by this plan, 50 of which were mammals. To be considered for the plan a species must be threatened or endangered in the wild, and a sufficient number of animals must exist to make captive breeding a viable solution. A coordinator for each species in the plan recommends a breeding regimen for each individual animal so that the greatest genetic diversity is maintained. Sometimes no breeding is recommended when there is no appropriate holding facility available for the offspring. Recently the scope of the SSP has been expanded to include research, education, and *in situ* conservation (including reintroduction—when feasible).

The captive okapi population remains small; just slightly over one hundred animals are held at the Epulu Compound and in a small number of widely spaced zoological facilities worldwide. Fourteen European zoos cooperate with the United States through their own plan, the Europais Ches Erhaltungszucht Program (European Breeding Preservation Program, EEP), while the SSP has fourteen facilities in the United States. Recently one facility in Japan has received okapis and is under the jurisdiction of the SSP. These protective organizations keep an International Studbook that is used in the management of the entire captive population. It contains data on individual animals, such as when and where the animal entered captivity or was born, its age, its parents (if known), its transfer history and the current institution where it resides, and (for deceased animals) the age at death and the cause. This record assists experts in making sound recommendations for the long-term maintenance of the okapi in captivity.

Rear view of okapi calf Zenzele.

Members of the EEP, the SSP, zoological institutions in other parts of the world, and several nongovernmental organizations have played important roles in the worldwide effort to preserve the okapi and to protect the Ituri Forest. For many years, this effort has centered around Epulu and has been subsidized by outside sources such as the Gilman Investment Company (White Oak Conservation Center, Yulee, Florida), the Wildlife Conservation Society (New York Zoological Society), regular donations from some SSP facilities, and fund-raising efforts by various zoological institutions. Primarily, funds have been used to provide support for conservation efforts, including research on other forest components, education of indigenous people, and attempts to protect the wild habitat.

Protected areas in Congo-Zaire are managed by the Institut Zairois pour la Conservation de la Natur (IZCN). Prior to 1992, seven national parks received varying degrees of protection: Virunga (established in 1925 and known for its population of mountain gorillas); Garamba (1938); Upemba (1939); and Salonga, Maiko (where some okapis are also found), Kahuzi-Biega, and Kundelungu, all established in 1970. In 1992 the government of Zaire significantly enlarged its network of protected areas with the creation of two new reserves. Mangrove National Park was established to protect the unique coastal and estuary mangrove systems on the Atlantic Coast at the mouth of the Zaire River. A government decree created the Réserve de Faune à Okapi (Okapi Wildlife Reserve), primarily to protect Zaire's endemic rain forest giraffe—the okapi—and its natural habitat. Also, a contract was negotiated by the Gilman Investment Company and the Wildlife Conservation Society with the government and IZCN to establish a center for research and training at the Epulu Compound— the Centre de Formation et de Recherche en Conservation Forestière.

The Okapi Wildlife Reserve covers a 1,372,625 hectare (ca. 3.4 million acres) section of the Ituri Forest—approximately one and a half times the size of Yellowstone National Park. In a 1996 paper, John Hart and Jefferson Hall estimated that the Okapi Wildlife Reserve harbored 3,900 to 6,350 okapis. It also is home to the largest population of Congo-Zaire's forest elephants and at least thirteen species of diurnal anthropoid primates—the highest diversity of these animals for a single site in Africa.

The primary, long-term objective of the Okapi Wildlife Refuge Management Plan is to "conserve and maintain in perpetuity the biologi-

Gray-cheeked mangabey.

cal diversity, ecological process and productivity of the Okapi Wildlife Reserve and associated ecosystems within the Ituri Forest and to ensure a continued reservoir of natural resources for sustainable exploitation by local people." Experts have indicated that in order for this goal to be attained, secondary objectives would need to be addressed. While natural ecosystems had garnered legal protection and efficient management, appropriate development projects and eco-tourism were needed to promote help for local communities and gather support for the conservation of the area's natural resources. A system of education and public awareness at every level of the community was needed to emphasize that the Ituri is a natural and national treasure. Meanwhile, research would continue to focus on the unique flora and fauna but would also encompass their relationship with the indigenous people.

The Wildlife Conservation Society and the Gilman Investment Company played a primary role initially in the establishment and maintenance of the Okapi Wildlife Reserve. Unfortunately, no funds existed in the government of Zaire's budget to support the reserve. All funds had to come from international sources. In 1994 a World Bank grant expired, leaving the IZCN station in Epulu with inadequate funds to manage the reserve. The base of operations for Rosemarie and Karl Ruf and the site of many ongoing research projects, Epulu Station was now in jeopardy. Many United States and European institutions holding captive okapis made substantial donations to help during the crisis. Monies were used for initial implementation of the management plan: to add guards, to outfit and support the education and public awareness team, for community development projects around the reserve, and for a vehicle used to patrol the reserve boundaries.

In 1997 a new regime came into power and the Democratic Republic of Congo was created. Like many third world countries, it faces numerous challenges. Those who protect Congo-Zaire's natural resources continue to deal with conversion of rain forest areas to pastoral grazing and agriculture land, deforestation, poaching, and illegal settlement.

Commercial logging is not prominent in the Okapi Wildlife Reserve, due primarily to the lack of sufficient road systems; however, slash-and-burn agriculture and harvesting of wood for sale is resulting in uncontrolled deforestation. Subsistence hunting for game meat, which is illegal within the reserve, probably does occur but is having only a minor impact on mammal populations (primarily small forest antelopes and primates). Commercial hunting on a large scale, for the sale of meat in towns, is much more detrimental. Other illegal exploitation includes mining for gold and diamonds.

Within the reserve, the primary concern today is immigration into the Bantu population. Immigrants place an ever-increasing demand on natural resources and threaten the traditional Mbuti-Bantu lifestyle.

Native hunter-gatherer pygmies, collectively known as the Mbuti, have long lived in the Ituri Forest and depended upon this ecosystem for their livelihood. Their traditional nomadic lifestyle does not negatively impact upon the forest. The Mbuti respect the importance of each species and the okapi, an animal which they revere, in particular. They recognize their dependence upon the forest and refer to it as "Father" or "Mother" because, like their parents, the Ituri provides food, shelter and clothing. The Mbuti also believe that the forest, like their parents, gives them affection. This sounds like a romantic idea put forth by some of the early writers on the Mbuti but, the pygmies have long been recognized for their special relationship with and knowledge of the forest.

Historically, the Mbuti have been closely associated with indigenous Bantu farmers who settled in isolated villages. The Bantus converted only small areas of the forest to their needs. Each group supplied needed resources for the other. Familiar with the forest, the Mbuti efficiently traded supplies such as bush meat from small game, wild mushrooms and honey for the Bantus' produce. The Mbuti also played important roles in village religious and rite-of-passage ceremonies. The new immigrants have no ongoing relationship with the forest or the Mbuti and their forest products. Conversion from a barter system to a cash system would negatively impact the Mbuti immensely.

Mbuti with leaves.

Gilman Investment Company's Epulu Okapi Project attempts to involve the Ituri people in the conservation of their home. An education initiative with the motto "Without Education, No Conservation" builds schools and utilizes a traveling school program which teaches children about the Okapi Wildlife Reserve and rain forest conservation. Mbuti pygmies are employed to gather the hundreds of pounds of leaves needed every day to feed the captive okapis at the compound. Bantu and Mbuti are employed in a variety of positions, including the support of eco-tourism. If the country's infrastructure improves, it is hoped that Epulu could once again become a major tourist destination in Eastern Congo-Zaire as it was in the 1950s. From the Epulu Project, the guards at the reserve receive supplements to their meager governmental salaries, food rations, and equipment, which enables them to more efficiently perform their duties of protecting the reserve.

Perhaps one of the most significant collaborations among Gilman Investment Company personnel, guards, and the local people is the capture of okapis as temporary founder stock for Epulu. Local villages have traditionally and deliberately left undisturbed areas known as "Zones de Capture," which harbor okapis. During a capture campaign, Gilman employs Mbuti and Bantu people associated with a particular "zone" to assist with the process. Food and medical care are provided to the village during the capture campaign. For each okapi captured in its "zone," the community is rewarded with a benefit it has selected. These may include a school, medical facility, bikes, or sewing machines. Such direct benefits and recognition that an okapi was captured near the community provides additional motivation for the people to continue to maintain these important ecological areas for the okapi and associated flora and fauna.

Just as it was when the Okapi Wildlife Reserve was created, limited resources are available from Congo-Zaire for its support and conservation. Worldwide cooperation among those interested in this World Heritage site will continue to be needed. Major support is being sought from a variety of international sources in order to provide long-term funding for operating and protecting the Okapi Wildlife Reserve. Unique partnerships, which are not directly influenced by national instability, have been forged to focus on the okapi as a flagship for conservation of rain forest biotas. Gilman Investment Company, the Wildlife Conservation Society, and SSP/EEP okapi facilities continue to make daily contributions to this effort. Proceeds from the purchase of this book will be used to protect okapi habitat in the Ituri Forest and thereby preserve the biodiversity of one of the last great rain forests in Africa. Donations to

Sun streaking through forest canopy onto a male okapi.

the Okapi Wildlife Reserve directly benefit both captive and wild okapi and many other species of plants and animals.

From the heart of Africa has come a beautiful and charismatic animal that has raised the awareness of those who have had the honor to be in its presence. Pursuit of knowledge about the okapi has led to many other discoveries about its unique home. As the okapi again disappears into the mist of the Ituri Forest, may we all work to preserve the living things that find refuge within it.

How Can You Help?

Tell your friends about the okapi and encourage them to learn more about this mysterious animal and its unique ecosystem.

Support and visit these institutions which provide okapis with a captive refuge:

Cheyenne Mountain Zoological Park, Colorado Springs, Colorado
Chicago Zoological Park, Brookfield, Illinois
Cincinnati Zoo and Botanical Garden, Cincinnati, Ohio
Columbus Zoological Park, Powell, Ohio
Dallas Zoo, Dallas, Texas
Denver Zoological Gardens, Denver, Colorado
Disney's Animal Kingdom, Kissimmee, Florida
International Wildlife Conservation Park, Bronx, New York
Oklahoma City Zoological Park, Oklahoma City, Oklahoma
Philadelphia Zoological Garden, Philadelphia, Pennsylvania
Saint Louis Zoological Park, St. Louis, Missouri
San Diego Wild Animal Park, Escondido, California
San Diego Zoological Garden, San Diego, California
White Oak Conservation Center, Yulee, Florida

Tzusuki Nature Park, Yokohama, Japan

Bristol Zoo Gardens, Bristol, Great Britain
Copenhagen Zoo, Frederiksberg, Denmark
Marwell Zoological Park, Hampshire, Great Britain
Münchener Tierpark Hellabrunn, Munich, Germany
Parc Zoologique de Paris, Paris, France
Royal Rotterdam Zoological and Botanical Gardens, Rotterdam, The
    Netherlands

Royal Zoological Society of Antwerp, Antwerp, Belgium
Wilhelma Zoologisch-Botanischer Garten, Stuttgart, Germany
The Zoological Society of London, London, Great Britain
Zoologischer Garten Basel, Basel, Switzerland
Zoologischer Garten Berlin, Berlin, Germany
Zoologischer Garten Köln, Cologne, Germany
Zoologischer Garten der Stadt Frankfurt am Main, Frankfurt am
    Main, Germany
Zoologischer Garten Wuppertal, Wuppertal, Germany

Assist efforts to preserve the okapi's native habitat and the Okapi Wildlife
Reserve. For more information contact:

Okapi Wildlife Reserve
c/o White Oak Conservation Center
3823 Owens Road
Yulee, Florida 32097
PHONE 904-225-3396
FAX 904-225-3337

THE END.

Selected Bibliography and Further Reading

The following list of titles indicates key references used in the preparation of this work and those recommended for further reading.

Barongi, R. A. 1985. Okapi and Epulu: a long term conservation project. *AAZPA Annual Conference Proceedings* 1985: 476–487. AAZPA, Oglebay, W. Va.

Beil, L. 1992. Infrasound of silence: Okapi may speak in tones humans can't hear. *Dallas Morning News,* December 21, 1992.

Bell, C. 1997. Wild cousins: okapis helping okapis. *Zoonooz* 70 (4): 9–13.

Benirschke, K. 1978. General survey of okapi pathology. *Acta Zoologica et Pathologica Antverpiensia* 71: 63–68.

Bennett, C. L., and S. L. Lindsey. 1989. Preliminary findings on the behavioral budgeting of two okapi calves during the first six months of life. *AAZPA Regional Conference Proceedings* 1989: 751–759. AAZPA, Oglebay, W. Va.

———. 1992. Some notes on the physiological and behavioral ontogeny of okapi (*Okapia johnstoni*) calves. *Zoo Biology* 11: 433–442.

Berg, J. K. 1982. Vocalization and associated behaviors of the African elephant (*Loxodonta africana*) in captivity. *Zeitschrift für Tierpsychologie* 63: 63–79.

Bodmer, R. E., and G. B. Rabb. 1985. Behavioral development and mother-infant relations in the forest giraffe *Okapia johnstoni.* In *Zoom Op Zoo,* ed. C. Kruyfhooft, pp. 33–53. Royal Zoological Society of Antwerp, Belgium.

———. 1992. *Okapia johnstoni.* American Society of Mammalogists Mammalian Species No. 422: 1–8.

Bourliere, F. 1964. *Natural history of mammals.* Knopf, New York. (English translation of 1913 edition.)

Chadwick, D. H. 1995. Ndoki: last place on earth. *National Geographic* 188 (1): 2–45

Chapin, J. R. 1948. How the Congo peacock was discovered. *Animal Kingdom* 51: 67–73.

Collar, N. J., and S. N. Stuart. 1985. Threatened birds of Africa and related islands. *ICBP/IUCN, Red Data Book,* Part 1: 182.

Cowen, R. 1990. Medicine on the wildside: animals may rely on a natural pharmacy. *Science News* 138 (18): 280–282.

Crandall, L. S. 1964. Family Giraffidae. In *Management of wild mammals in captivity,* pp. 606–625. University of Chicago Press, Chicago.

Crissey, S. D. 1991. Okapi handrearing: okapi milk data. MS on file, Chicago Zoological Society, Brookfield.

Dagg, A. I. 1960a. Gaits of the giraffe and okapi. *Journal of Mammalogy* 41 (2): 282.

———. 1960b. The role of the neck in the movements of the giraffe. *Journal of Mammalogy* 43 (1): 88–97.

Dagg, A. I., and J. B. Foster. 1976. *The giraffe: its biology, behavior and ecology.* Van Nostrand Reinhold, New York.

De Bois, H., and B. Van Puijenbroeck. 1992. *Studbook of the okapi.* Royal Zoological Society of Antwerp, Belgium.

De Bois, H., B. Van Puijenbroeck, and A. A. Dhondt. 1988. The studbook population of the okapi *Okapia johnstoni*: some remarks on the current demographic and population genetic status. *Acta Zoologica et Pathologica Antverpiensia* 80: 53–64.

Delacour, J. 1957. *Guide to the pheasants of the world.* Allen Publishing Co., Salt Lake City, Utah.

Dorst, J., and P. Dandelot. 1980. *Large mammals of Africa: a field guide.* William Collins Sons and Co., Glasgow, Scotland.

Durham, M. 1997. Journey to Epulu. *Zoonooz* 70 (4): 14–18.

Gatti, A. 1937. The strangest animal in Africa. *Travel* 68 (6): 11–16.

Gijzen, A. 1959. *Das Okapi* Okapia johnstoni *(Sclater).* Die Neue Brehm-Bücherei, A. Ziemsen Verlag, Wittenberg.

Gosse, P. H. 1861. *The romance of natural history.* Gould and Lincoln, Boston.

Gotch, A. F. 1979. *Mammals—their Latin names explained: a guide to animal classification.* Blandford Press, Poole Dorset.

Grzimek, H. C. B. 1972. The okapi. *Grzimek's Animal Encyclopedia* 13: 247–254. Van Nostrand Reinhold, New York.

———. 1990. The giraffe. *Grzimek's encyclopedia of mammals* 13: 255–266. Van Nostrand Reinhold, New York.

Hart, J. A. 1991. Forage selection, forage availability and use of space by okapi *Okapia johnstoni.* Paper presented at Ungulates 1991 Institut de recherche sur les grands mammiferes, Universite Paul Sabatier, Toulouse, France.

Hart, J., and J. Hall. 1996. Status of eastern Zaire's forest parks and reserves. *Conservation Biology* 10 (2): 316–327.

Hart, J., and T. Hart. 1984. The Mbuti of Zaire: political change and the opening of the Ituri Forest. *Cultural Survival Quarterly* 8 (3): 18–20.

———. 1988a. A summary report on the behaviour, ecology and conservation of the okapi (*Okapia johnstoni*) in Zaire. *Acta Zoologica et Pathologica Antverpiensia* 80: 19–28.

———. 1988b. Tracking the rainforest giraffe. *Animal Kingdom* 91: 26–32.

———. 1989. Ranging and feeding behavior of okapi (*Okapia johnstoni*) in the Ituri forest of Zaire: food limitation in a rain-forest herbivore? In *Symposia of the Zoological Society of London,* Vol. 61: *The biology of large African mammals in their environment,* ed. P. A. Jewell and G. M. O. Maloiy, pp. 31–50. Zoological Society of London.

———. 1992. Between sun and shadow. *Natural History* 101 (11): 28–35.

Horwich, R., C. Kitchen, M. Wangel, and R. Ruthe. 1983. Behavioral development in okapis and giraffes. *Zoo Biology* 2: 105–125.

Hutchins, M. 1991. *1990–1991 AAZPA annual report on conservation and science.* 1st ed. AAZPA, Oglebay, W. Va.

Hutchinson, J. 1954. *Flora of west tropical Africa.* Vol. 1, Part 1. Crown Agents for Oversea Governments and Administrations, London.

Jaspers, R., and F. De Vree. 1978. Trends in the development of the skull of *Okapia johnstoni* (Sclater, 1901). *Acta Zoologica et Pathologica Antverpiensia* 71: 107–130.

Johnston, H. 1900. Letter from Sir Harry Johnston from Uganda. *Proceedings of the Zoological Society of London,* August 21, 1900.

———. 1902. *The Uganda Protectorate.* Vol. 2. Hutchinson & Co., London.

———. 1906. The okapi. In *The living animals of the world,* ed. C. J. Cornish, pp. 267–270. Hutchinson & Co., London.

———. 1923. *The story of my life.* Bobbs-Merrill Co., Indianapolis.

Kingdon, J. 1979a. Giraffids. *East African mammals* 3 (Part B): 308–337. Academic Press, New York.

———. 1979b. Okapi. *East African mammals* 3 (Part B): 338–345. Academic Press, New York.

———. 1989. *Island Africa: an evolutionary whirlpool—the Zaire Basin.* Princeton University Press, Princeton, N.J.

Lang, H. 1918. In quest of the rare okapi. *New York Zoological Society Bulletin* 21 (3): 1601–1614.

Lankester, E. R. 1901a. On *Okapia johnstoni. Proceedings of the Zoological Society of London* 1901 (2): 279–281.

———. 1901b. On *Okapia,* a new genus of Giraffidae from Central Africa. *Proceedings of the Zoological Society of London* 1901 (2): 472–474.

———. 1902a. The specific name of the okapi represented by Sir Harry Johnston to the British Museum. *Annals of Natural History* 7: 417–418.

———. 1902b. On *Okapia,* a new genus of Giraffidae from Central Africa. *Transactions of the Zoological Society of London* 16 (6): 279–314.

———. 1903. Hair whorls in the okapi. *Proceedings of the Zoological Society of London* 1903 (2): 337–340.

———. 1908. On certain points in the structure of the cervical vertebrae of the okapi and the giraffe. *Proceedings of the Zoological Society of London,* 1908: 320–334.

Lindsey, S. L., and C. L. Bennett. 1991. Mother-infant relationships and the behavioral budgeting of four okapi (*Okapia johnstoni*) calves during the first six months of life. Report to the Animal Behavior Society at the annual meeting, Wilmington, North Carolina.

Lindsey, S. L, C. L. Bennett, J. J. Fried, and J. Pritchard. 1993. Functional analysis of infrasound in the okapi (*Okapia johnstoni*): mother-infant communication. *AAZPA Annual Conference Proceedings,* 1993: 299–303. AAZPA, Oglebay, W. Va.

Lindsey, S. L., C. L. Bennett, E. Pyle, M. Willow, and A. Yang. 1994. Calf management and the collection of physiological data for okapi. *International Zoo Yearbook* 33: 263–268.

Loskutoff, N. M., J. E. Ott, and B. L. Lasley. 1982. Urinary steroid evaluation to monitor ovarian function in exotic ungulates. I. Pregnanediol-3–glucuronide immunoreactivity in the okapi (*Okapia johnstoni*). *Zoo Biology* 1: 45–53.

Lukas, J. 1993. Conservation in action: Okapi/Epulu Project. *Karatasi,* no. 1 (Summer 1993). White Oak Conservation Center, Yulee, Fla.

MacClintock, D. 1973. The okapi—a close relative of the giraffe's. In *The natural history of giraffes,* pp. 115–123. Scribner, New York.

Major, C. J. F. 1902a. Note on the okapi. *Proceedings of the Zoological Society of London* 1902 (2): 73–79.

———. 1902b. On a specimen of okapi lately received at Brussels. *Proceedings of the Zoological Society of London* 1902 (2): 339–350.

Mark, J. 1995. *The king of the world in the land of the pygmies.* University of Nebraska Press, Lincoln.

Miller, P. 1995. Jane Goodall. *National Geographic* 188 (6): 102–129.

Miller Ben Shaul, D. 1962. The composition of the milk of wild animals. *International Zoo Yearbook* 4: 333–342.

Nlamba, J., and J. Lukas. 1994. Epulu update: management plan for Okapi Wildlife Reserve approved. *Karatasi,* no. 6–7 (Fall 1994). White Oak Conservation Center, Yulee, Fla.

Payne, K. B., W. R. Langbauer, Jr., and E. M. Thomas. 1986. Infrasonic calls of the Asian elephant (*Elaphas maximus*). *Behavioral Ecology and Sociobiology* 18: 297–301.

Pearson, H., and A. Wright. 1968. Some observations on the rearing of an okapi calf, *Okapia johnstoni. International Zoo Yearbook* 8: 134–136.

Pellew, R. A. 1984. Giraffe and okapi. In *The encyclopedia of mammals,* ed. D. Mcdonald, pp. 534–541. Facts on File, New York.

Petit, P., and W. De Meurichy. 1986. On the chromosomes of the okapi, *Okapia johnstoni. Annales de Génetique* 29 (4):232–234.

Petric, A. 1987. Okapi management. *AAZPA Regional Conference Proceedings,* 1987: 566–571. AAZPA, Oglebay, W. Va.

Pocock, R. I. 1936. Preliminary note on a new point in the structure of the feet of the okapi. *Proceedings of the Zoological Society of London,* May 19, 1936, 583–586.

Poole, J. H., and C. J. Moss. 1989. Elephant mate searching: group dynamics and vocal and olfactory communication. In *Symposia of the Zoological Society of London,* Vol. 61: *The biology of large African mammals in their environment,* ed. P. A. Jewell and G. M. O. Maloiy, pp. 111–125. Zoological Society of London.

Putnam, A. E. 1954. *Madami.* Prentice-Hall, New York.

Pyle, E., and M. Willow. 1991. Management of okapi calves (*Okapia johnstoni*) at the Dallas Zoo. *AAZPA Regional Conference Proceedings,* 1991: 399–406. AAZPA, Oglebay, W. Va.

Rabb, G. B. 1978. Birth, early behavior and clinical data on the okapi. *Acta Zoologica et Pathologica Antverpiensia* 71: 93–105.

Raphael, B. L. 1988. Neonatal illness characterized by dermatitis, hyperthermia and anemia in an okapi. *Acta Zoologica et Pathologica Antverpiensia* 80: 43–52.

Raphael, B. L., L. Sneed, and J. Ott-Joslin. 1986. Rotavirus-like infection associated with diarrhea in okapi. *Journal of the American Veterinary Medical Association* 189: 1183–1184.

Reason, R. C. 1991. Preliminary observations on growth and development in the okapi *Okapia johnstoni* at Brookfield Zoo, Chicago. *International Zoo Yearbook* 30: 216–219.

Reynolds, R. J. III. 1987. The only circus okapis. *Bandwagon,* March–April, 18–22.

Saambili, K., and K. Ruf. 1995. Food and water intake variations during lactation periods of two okapi at the Epulu Station. *Epulu Update,* March 1995, 5. White Oak Conservation Center, Yulee, Fla.

Saambili, K., N. Ndjaikpa, and J. Lukas. 1994. Returning a male okapi to the wild from Epulu Station. *Epulu Update,* September 1994, 7. White Oak Conservation Center, Yulee, Fla.

Savage, R. J. G., and M. R. Long. 1986. *Mammal evolution: an illustrated guide.* Facts on File, New York.

Schildkrout, E., and C. A. Keim. 1990. *African reflections: art from northeastern Zaire.* American Museum of Natural History, New York.

Schwankl, B., and J. Berg. 1988. Animal of mystery: the okapi. *Zoonooz* 62 (9): 4–9.

Schwarzenberger, F., M. Patzl, R. Francke, A. Ochs, R. Buiter, W. Schaftenaar, and W. De Meurichy. 1993. Fecal progestagen evaluations to monitor the estrous cycle and pregnancy in the okapi (*Okapia johnstoni*). *Zoo Biology* 12: 549–559.

Schwarzenberger, F., W. Rietschel, W. Schaftenaar, P. Bircher, K. Leus, and B. Van Puijenbroeck. 1997. An overview of 6 years of faecal progestagen evaluations in the okapi (*Okapi johnstoni*). *Verh. ber. Erkrg. Zootiere.* 38: 163–168.

Sclater, P. L. 1901. On an apparently new species of zebra from the Semliki forest. *Proceedings of the Zoological Society of London* 1901 (1): 50–52.

―――. 1904. Report on visit to Brussels to examine okapi specimens. *Proceedings of the Zoological Society of London* 1904 (2): 180–181.

―――. 1906. Letter of Capt. P. H. G. Powell-Cotton, F. Z. S., about the okapi (*Okapia johnstoni*). *Proceedings of the Zoological Society of London* 1906 (2): 760–761.

Senft, B. 1978. Immunologic aspects in artificial raising of newborn okapi. *Acta Zoologica et Pathologica Antverpiensia* 71: 53–58.

Shurter, S., and P. Foster-Turley. 1996. *Proceedings of the Okapi Metapopulation Workshop.* White Oak Conservation Center, Yulee, Fla.

Singer, R., and E. L. Bone. 1960. Modern giraffes and fossil giraffes of Africa. *Annals of the South African Museum* 45: 375–548.

Spinage, C. A. 1968. The okapi—sole relative of the giraffe. In *The book of the giraffe,* pp. 143–161. Collins, London.

Stanley, H. M. 1890. *In darkest Africa.* 2 vols. Sampson Low, Marston. Searle and Rivington, Ltd., London.

Turnbull, C. M. 1965. *Wayward servants: the two worlds of the African pygmies.* Natural History Press, Garden City, New York.

Urban, K. E., C. H. Fry, and S. Keith. 1986. *The birds of Africa.* Vol.2, II. Academic Press, London.

Van Puijenbroeck, B., and H. DeBois, eds. 1989. *SSP/EEP masterplan workshop: okapi.* Royal Zoological Society of Antwerp, Belgium.

Van Puijenbroeck, B., and K. Leus. 1996. *Okapi* Okapia johnstoni *International Studbook, 31 December 1996.* Royal Society of Antwerp.

Vaughan, T. A. 1978. *Mammalogy.* W. B. Sanders Co., Philadelphia.

Von Muggenthaler, E. K., J. W. Stoughton, and J. C. Daniel, Jr. 1993. Infrasound from the Rhinocerotidae. In *Rhinoceros biology and conservation,* ed. O. A. Ryder, pp. 136–140. Zoological Society of San Diego.

Walther, F. 1962. Über ein Speil bei *Okapia johnstoni. Zietschrift für Säugetierkunde* 27: 245–251.

————. 1984. *Communication and expression in hoofed mammals.* Indiana University Press, Bloomington.

Weise, R. J., and M. Hutchins. 1994. *Species Survival Plans: strategies for wildlife conservation.* American Zoo and Aquarium Association, Wheeling, West Va.

Wexo, J. B. 1982. *Giraffe.* Zoo Books. Wildlife Education, Ltd., San Diego.

William, J. G., and N. Arlott. 1981. *Birds of East Africa: a field guide.* Collins Press, London.

Index

Italic page numbers indicate illustrations.